SEEDS OF DECADENCE IN THE LATE NINETEENTH-CENTURY NOVEL

SEEDS OF DECADENCE
IN THE LATE NINETEENTH-CENTURY NOVEL

A Crisis in Values

Suzanne Nalbantian

First published 1983 by
THE MACMILLAN PRESS LTD
London and Basingstoke
Companies and representatives
throughout the world

ISBN 0 333 24638 1

Typeset in Great Britain by
Wessex Typesetters Ltd
Frome, Somerset

Printed in Hong Kong

To Anna B. and Stepan Nalbantian, my parents

Contents

Preface

This book grew from my fascination with certain compelling writers of a hundred years ago who foresaw some of the dilemmas which were to continue into our present age. Having written a book, *The Symbol of the Soul from Hölderlin to Yeats*, about the shift in sensitivity from the nineteenth to the twentieth century, I became further interested in the way this transition affected the novel form in what I found to be the most critical period of that change. I was drawn to a group of writers whose first merit was their arresting power of expression. I set out to extract them from the standard literary classifications imposed upon them in their national contexts – to discover an affiliation as a basis for a comparative literary study. The reading of these books from a socio-aesthetic perspective focuses on what they collectively contributed to a spirit and a style, revealing the intensity of their authors' concern for Western man.

A specific trip provided an inspiration for this work. In June 1978, I journeyed to the Hardy country of Dorset in the company of my brother Haig Nalbantian, who had recently terminated an honours essay on Hardy and who had communicated to me his insights on the philosophical complexity of the author. We virtually traced the paths of heath and furze which entangle that countryside. The impressions of that trip were startling. It was as if the landscape were staged: a dead black crow appeared on one of our paths (evoking the perplexity of young Jude), a sudden storm broke out on Egdon Heath trapping us amidst fallen trees and sidelong gulfs, an ink-like pitch blackness penetrated the surroundings of the inn where we were staying, and an old man in a local pub, who appeared like a relic from the past, gave us first-hand impressions of Hardy.

I wish to thank my publisher, Mr Tim Farmiloe, who upon the publication of my first book asked me to submit a proposal for another. His constant care and extraordinary civility following the course of this book have been invaluable.

I am appreciative of the support and encouragement which I have been given by both the Department of English and the Administration of C. W. Post College, Long Island University. The Trustee Award for Scholarly Achievement, which was recently presented to me, served as a catalyst to the completion of this book. I also am grateful to Dean Maithili Schmidt and Professors Arthur Coleman and S. C. V. Stetner for authorizing the provision of essential logistical arrangements.

In conducting the research for this book, I was assisted by the staffs of several libraries. I would like to acknowledge in particular the Library of Congress, Hofstra University Library in Long Island and the Fales Collection of New York University.

Finally, special thanks to Ms Anita Silk for her careful and caring work on the final typescript.

Old Westbury
Long Island   S. N.

1 The Grammar of Decadence: Perversity, Paradox and Perplexity

The seeds of Decadence* were sown in the transitional period in Western literature from 1870 to 1900. To associate the word simply with the Aesthetes of the 1890s is reductive because Decadence was not Aestheticism but an aesthetic of transition expressing a crisis in values and language in the Western world. Nor was this a conscious programme as fashioned by the literary schools of the time, for it emerged unconsciously in the texture of the prose of major novelists of the period extremely sensitive to the gruelling moral traumas over and above their literary allegiances.

The meaning of the term as here perceived seems most gravely ingrained in the chief writings of such prominent novelists as Fyodor Dostoevsky, Henry James, Emile Zola, Thomas Hardy and Joseph Conrad, names not ordinarily identified with decadence or necessarily associated with each other. The moral maze of a society in transition and change is crystallized in the personal perversities, paradoxes and perplexities of individual protaganists in key novels of these authors from Dostoevsky's Idiot to Conrad's Kurtz.

Strangely, the theoreticians of the standard term 'decadence' turned to a more partial and popular meaning of the word. Aware of 'decadence' as an epithet from mid-century on, literary critics, poets and philosophers created a cumulative connotation. They reached a consensus that the age was 'decadent' and enacted an ensuing commentary and exploration of a term groping for definition.

A resounding philosophic expression of decadence is obviously found in the thought of Nietzsche, who wrote at the very heart of

---

* Decadence written with a capital D designates the meaning of the term as proposed by this study.

1

the period and who became the self-ordained philosopher of decadence. His outright divestiture of traditional Western moral criteria is the framework in which the identification of the term emerged. In the Nietzschean idiom decadence – a word used obsessively throughout his writings – denotes the 'naïve' Christian, specifically Pauline mentality which had evolved from the Judaic world and was based on an 'erroneous' dualism. It was associated with the human and declining (*niedergehend*) life and exemplified in the precarious existence of the tightrope walker who falls between the subhuman and superhuman: poles which Nietzsche envisaged outside the context of that decline. What Nietzsche communicated figuratively in the 'last man' of the intentionally prophetic *Thus Spoke Zarathustra* (1883–5) and more directly in his other writings is the death of *moral man*, reiterated and emphasized by Michel Foucault in his notion of 'the absolute dispersion of man'.[1] This admission is even more *heaven-shaking* than the better known statement regarding the death of God.

Personally nurtured in a Lutheran tradition, Nietzsche battled against such decadent tendencies within himself, admitting that he was a child of a decadent age and struggling against what he regarded as weakness and impoverishment of vital life forces.[2] When Nietzsche takes a virulent stand against his former friend Wagner, the object of his attack is in fact the *Parsifal* opera. He views the composer as attempting to overcome the apocalyptic stance of the *Götterdämmerung* by resorting to a Christian ending. Nietzsche had great disdain for the pristine knight of 'idiotic' purity.

The discussion of the word 'noble' (*vornehm*) became the focal point of Nietzsche's transvaluation after the pronouncement of the devaluation of God. Nietzsche offered a whole new set of correlatives for the communication of the stimulus 'noble', such as arrogance and egoism. He forcefully demonstrated the obsolescence of the formerly Christian-oriented connotations of purity, justice, self-denial, sacrifice, humility, forgiveness, charity and pity. Designating such values as corrupt, through a verbal act of inversion he challenged the moral and aesthetic standards established and accepted by European civilization.

In the literary context, *Thus Spoke Zarathustra* is the most significant work of Nietzsche because of its stylistic connection with Decadence. The Persian persona, Zarathustra, who engages in a devastatingly sardonic diatribe against previously accepted word-concepts, explicitly and implicitly attacks the language which had harboured the decadent values: 'Rather, that you, my friends, might grow weary of the old words you have learned from the fools and the liars.'[3] Nietzsche viewed those old words in terms of toys (*Spielwerke*) which were carried away into the depths of the sea, but Zarathustra consoles his crying followers, whom he considers as naïve children, by saying: 'you, too, my friends, shall have your comfortings – and – new colorful shells [*neue bunte Muscheln*]'.[4]

Nietzsche associated the 'old words' with all the mire and confusion of the rabble (*Gisendel*) that poisoned and degraded the language:

> Life is a well of joy; but where the rabble drinks too, all wells are poisoned. I am fond of all that is clean, but I have no wish to see the grinning snouts and the thirst of the unclean. . . . They have poisoned the holy water with their lustfulness; and when they called their dirty dreams pleasure, they poisoned the language too.[5]

In his ironic and devastatingly playful medium, he modifies the rejected word-values by their contextual pejoratives, perversely using the standard lexicon of morality with the effect of linguistically obliterating it. Cunningly, he uses the tenor of the moralist to nullify the morality. He suggests by *Gesindel* both the physical crowd and the confused jargon or nonsense of previous ideograms. In an extremely vivid and sensorial expression, he identifies the previous words as debris, putrid and rotting, maggot-eaten and decayed: 'And, holding my nose, I walked disgruntled through all of yesterday and today: verily, all of yesterday and today smells foul of the writing rabble.'[6] Both in his use of his own native German and in his simulation of Biblical structures of parable, he plays upon the moralistically connotative character of the physical word 'dirt' to suggest the sordidness of the 'moral'; as a striking gesture he holds his nose to dramatize what he regards as the putrefaction of the previously established moral connotations.

In his recognition and demonstration of decayed values within the context of critical change, Nietzsche mixed the moral with the linguistic: 'we are not rid of God because we still have faith in grammar.'[7] He thereby suggested that a new morality required a new language. He was out to destroy its pristine meanings by making connotative and figurative substitutions, replete with

metaphors and neologisms. As it is reputed, his final stance is that
of an iconoclast, annihilating idols established by his Western
heritage. Among those which sounded hollow are such absolutes
as unity, identity, permanence, substance, cause, thinghood,
being. And Nietzsche perceived the dimming of these idols
(*Götzendämmerung*) not so much through the eye as through the
ear, which is his central vehicle or metaphor of scrutiny. His
soundboard was language and his philosophic ear detected false
intonation therein. The ironic tone and the jesting quality of
Zarathustra, visually highlighted by the buffoon in motley who
pushes the 'last man' off the tightrope, undermine and at the same
time overcome the metaphysical decadence through the instru-
ment of a Decadent style.

The midday hour or noon, as expressed in *Thus Spoke
Zarathustra*, transfixes Decadence as transition. For Nietzsche
decadence is both an ending and a beginning. His idiosyncratic
interpretation foreshadowed an ideology of decadence, associated
with a cultural process and what he regarded as the evolution of
Western man. For this reason Nietzsche welcomed the excessive-
ness of decadence (*Steigerung der décadence*) in an oxymoronic
expression in *The Antichrist*.

In the context of literary criticism, the use of the term became
predominant in nineteenth-century France and contributed to its
popular identification with Latinism and excess. Through the
century, the word began to accrue meanings as it shifted from a
term designating the decline of a culture to the identification of a
style. Its original referential meaning was to Latin literature.[8] The
'decadence' alluded to was the historical fall of Roman civilization, as previously brought to attention by Montesquieu and
Gibbon. In this frame of reference the conservative neo-classical
critic, Désiré Nisard, writing *Poètes latins de la décadence* (1834)
began to define decadence as a style *in a pejorative and
derogatory tone* and put the word as such in circulation. He
viewed it as a romanticism, associating it with the late Latin
period and with particular writers such as Lucan. Nisard noted
the literary manifestations of such a cultural 'fall' in the writings
of the late Latins whose style he found to be too ornamental and
embellished. He especially referred to Lucan's *Pharsalia* with its
ornate descriptions, its materialistic aspect and the cult of the
ugly based on a predilection for realistic precision.

A mythology of Latinized decadence was appropriated by poets of the second half of the nineteenth century, particularly by those in France. Conceptually they seemed compelled to announce in declarative statements that decadence was a basic undercoating of their poetic attitudes. Even Mallarmé, withdrawn and abstinent in life style, has this sense of a Roman surfeit and overindulgence in his overwhelming and contagious cry in the first line of 'Brise marine': 'La chair est triste, hélas! et j'ai lu tous les livres', as if to qualify an historical moment when man has seen all, experienced all and read all. Hence his poetic task was to cultivate sensuality theoretically. The satyr-like Verlaine, on the other hand, was more overt in establishing *the* analogy between the Second French Empire and the late Latin one when he viewed his weariness symptomatically in his sonnet 'Langueur' (1883): 'Je suis l'Empire à la fin de la décadence.'

There is also another historical reference to decadence that creeps into poetic usage. For instance, Théophile Gautier, the Parnassian poet-critic, reveals a shift in emphasis from the Latin to the Byzantine. The word becomes associated with the paradoxical connotation of maturity and ripeness (over-ripeness?) coupled with immanent weariness and spectacular decline. In his Preface (1868) to Baudelaire's *Les Fleurs du mal*, he described this 'decadent' style.

> This style of decadence is the last word of the Word summoned to express everything and then pushed to its extreme. One can recall, in this connection, the language which was already marbled by the greenness of decomposition and as if decayed from the late Roman Empire and the complicated refinements of the Byzantine school, the last form of Greek art fallen in deliquescence: but such is indeed the necessary and fatal idiom of peoples and civilizations whose natural life has been replaced by an artificial [*factice*] one.[9]

The use of the exquisite word *déliquescence* suggests Gautier's positive predisposition for what he observed as Byzantine style and refinement. It is something which the minor stylists who established the notion of *décadisme* and contributed to Anatole Baju's periodical *Le Décadent* (1886–9) attempted to emulate. It describes the ornate idiom and the clichés of the Rhymers' Club in England (1890–5). Contrivances in language were sought to provide delights and new stimulations for the *blasés* of a world-weary age. The word *factice* emphasizes the intentional artificiality of the decadent style in its first associations with Aestheticism. Gautier also referred to the fact that the new style is complex and typified by technical vocabulary: learned and *recherché*, with new terms drawn from cosmetics, chemistry, medicine, psychology.

From mid-century on, first in France and then in England, it is a fact that the term 'decadence' acquired its specific literary association with the Art for Art's Sake movement and the Aesthetes. The two major novels of decadence were recognized as J. K. Huysmans's *A Rebours* (1884) and Oscar Wilde's *The Picture of Dorian Gray* (1891). They are identified in their respective countries as *the* 'decadent' novels; they are textually linked in the fact that Dorian is engrossed in the reading of what Wilde describes as the so-called French yellow book. *A Rebours* was to be called 'the Breviary of the Decadence' by the English critic Arthur Symons in his book on Oscar Wilde. In fact Huysmans himself discussed the nature of this 'decadence' in a preface written twenty years after the publication of his book.[10] He explained that his target had been a rampant Naturalism. In envisaging his work as a blow to Naturalism through his escape into artifice and distillation of feeling and sensations, actually he had proceeded to *denaturalize* language and create literary language for the expression of the perverse. Hence the title, 'Against the Grain'.

In this novel without a plot, it has been observed that the single character, Des Esseintes, has many of the accoutrements of the decadent Aesthete, stereotyped in terms of his noble heritage (he is the *last* scion of a noble line), his isolated demesne, his hypersensitivity and nervous propensity (the standard psychological condition of such a specimen), his decaying teeth, his absolute disgust with life and progeniture, and his indulgence in new sensations and refuge in ratiocination to counter his dire sense of boredom. It is interesting that the artificial life-style, which the character Des Esseintes is presumed to be cultivating in his retreat in his country house in Fontenay, is paralleled by an art-style where the perverse is substituted for the natural. Language is itself conceived as a life organism in decay and salvaged by the artistic contrivances of the hero. From this reading of the book a Decadent syntax of extracts emerges, a prose drawn from experiments with a gamut of new sensations dissociated from what Huysmans regarded as the natural and decaying world before him, and communicated through a sensuous-concrete vocabulary. This is comparable to Nietzsche's development of a language capable of conveying moral turpitude.

In this ironical chronicle of decomposition, Des Esseintes masters the syntax of odours, sensations and colours as he focuses paradoxically upon *the most natural symbol of perversity*: the flower. In his attraction to flora, the art-like specimens of the natural world (in chapter 8), he illustrates most literally the perversity of his programme. In general, the flower is nature's manifestation of beauty, and in his role of aesthete it is natural that Des Esseintes would surround himself with aesthetic specimens. His first step, however, is to defy the natural flower by substituting for it the challenges of an artificial one; seemingly satisfying his 'penchant naturel vers l'artifice'.[11] But that perverse inclination toward the artificial leads to a further act of defiance and deviation. Locating the perverse within nature itself he arrives at the ultimate act of inversion: 'After the artificial [*factice*] flowers mimicking the genuine flowers, he wanted natural flowers imitating false flowers.'[12]

Here there is a shift to a new lexicon of artifice-like signifiers drawn from nature itself. Naming nature and defying it simultaneously, he locates the most monstrous and the rarest flowers in the state of botany of his time such as orchids and calladiums. These perversely defy nature by their semblance of artificiality: their glossy, wax-like surfaces, resembling artificial rather than natural materials, seemingly fabricated of cloth, paper, porcelain or metal. Most striking of these is the infamous cattleya, bell-shaped, lilac in colour, exuding an odour of deal and accepted as a magnificent toy. Through the power of association and process of materialization the flowers are transmuted into monstrous metaphors which permeate the entire chapter and are interfaced with anatomical structures of living being (undersides of lips, hearts, throats), visceral organs exuding viscous fluids, membranes, sexual orifices. These metonymies produce a culminating hyperbole of perversity in a sexual context: the vision of the syphilitic woman or Pox (*la Grande Vérole*). Hence the flowers become the transmitters of disease, concretely conveying the notion of decay. Although Huysmans was presumably confronting Naturalism, he was in fact showing how decadence was directly related to Naturalism.

It is most appropriate, then, that of flora and fauna the orchid became in fact the popularized symbol of the decadent aestheticism. It became the password for the Decadents, processed by Huysmans, satirized by Mallarmé (*le trop grand glaïeul*) in a poem responding to Huysmans's portrayal of Des Esseintes as a prototype,[13] and appropriated by Symons (who in a poem from the cycle 'Violet' said: 'the orchid mostly is the flower I love,/. . . artificial flower of my ideal'), by Aubrey Beardsley (who was dubbed by Symons as a monstrous orchid), by d'Annunzio (prominently in his *Il Piacere* (*The Child of Pleasure*) and eventually by Proust (who makes the cattleya a sign for the *art* of love-making in *Du Côté de chez Swann*) – to give some of the most striking examples I have observed.

At one point, Huysmans makes his character the direct spokesman for the 'decadent' Aestheticism as he transparently alludes to Nisard's pejorative valuation of Latin decadence and rebuffs it; he retaliates by admiring the very authors whom Nisard had condemned, including Lucan. Des Esseintes is even made to go so far as to voice a literary critical viewpoint in making an analogy between the Latin decadent and the decadent of his own times, and relishing what Huysmans regards as the decomposition of the French language, a language ready to expire in ecstasy: 'It was the death-throes of the old language which after having become moldy century after century, was finally dissolving by reaching the deliquium of the Latin language.'[14] But in the guise of Des Esseintes there is no sustained pursuit of this notion; he is carried away by it until the novelty wears off as a source of immoral attraction.

It is obvious that like *A Rebours*, *The Picture of Dorian Gray* also contained a decadent stereotype. In fact Symons called Wilde 'The perfect representative of all that is meant by the word "decadence" as used in the "nineties" of [the] last century'.[15] If Huysmans had *de*naturalized expression, Wilde *super*naturalized it through the uncanny superiority he had attributed to the aesthetic object over human life in the novel. The artefact was appropriately at the centre of observation and objectified the inner excesses as well as the visible indulgences of the behaviour of the dandy. The supernatural quality that the portrait acquires is an aggregate of the characteristics that had been identified as 'decadent' in the world of reality. Although the critical statement that the murder of Basil Hallward (the artist–creator of the portrait) is 'the murder of Pre-Raphaelite Art and Ruskinian

"Moral Aesthetic" by decadent art"[16] sounds academic, there is
historical validity in the use of the term 'decadent' to express an
aesthetic process rather than merely a moral one.

Ironically, Wilde, whose aestheticism might be viewed as
'decadent', passes the label along to the Naturalists in his
dialectical dialogue 'The Decay of Lying' (1889). The word
'decay' in this title is attributed to the Naturalist and Realistic
tendencies of the day: 'The third stage is when Life gets the upper
hand, and drives Art out into the wilderness. This is the true
decadence, and it is from this that we are now suffering.'[17] In
using the term to describe verisimilitude, he dissociates it from
Aestheticism and assigns it to writers such as James, Zola and
Maupassant but for reasons that are not those discernible as
constituting Decadence in this study. For Wilde, 'decadence'
means a dearth of imaginative distortion and contrivance in art.
But in identifying it with the moral turpitudes that such writers
presumably convey 'realistically' in their fiction, he uses the word
in an evaluative rather than in a stylistic way. He thereby puts
himself in an aesthetically embarrassing position. For, ultimately,
in his categorical bias against Naturalist prose, Wilde refused to
see the symbolism inherent in the greater Naturalists and Realists
of his time, whose Decadence (as will be seen) lay precisely in
their departure from the 'mimetic' norm and *not* in their total
adherence to it, as Wilde would have it.

It was the English literary critic, Arthur Symons, who
notably attempted to turn the word into a descriptive term to
designate the emergence of a new modern style. In his famous
article entitled 'The Decadent Movement in Literature', which
first appeared in *Harper's New Monthly Magazine* in November
1893, Symons announced the existence of a new literary movement emanating from France and rising above the older classifications of Romantic and Classic:

> The most representative literature of the day – the writing
> which appeals to, which has done so much to form the younger
> generation – is certainly not classic, nor has it any relation with
> that old antithesis of the Classic, the Romantic. After a fashion
> it is no doubt a decadence: it has all the qualities that we find in
> the Greek, the Latin decadence: an intense self-consciousness,
> a restless curiosity in research, an over-subtilizing refinement
> upon refinement, a spiritual and moral perversity.[18]

In an impressionistic way, Symons characterized 'decadence' as that which was 'beautifully, curiously poisonous'[19] in modern art and used it as a broad rubric to encompass both Symbolism and Impressionism. This encompassing category included such writers as Verlaine, Mallarmé, Maeterlinck, Villiers de l'Isle-Adam, the Goncourt Brothers and Huysmans. It is interesting to note that the title was later altered to the book title *The Symbolist Movement in Literature* (1899) as the word 'decadence' incurred increasingly pejorative connotation and notoriety in English circles. In the later work, Symons turned to the Symbolist poetic mode as the 'Ideal of Decadence'. In making this shift in terminology, Symons inadvertently was associating new usages of language in the 'great' poetry of the period with the more appropriate rubric of Symbolism.

The fate of the two major English decadent journals also contributed to Symons's ultimate rejection of the term. *The Yellow Book* and *The Savoy* underwent increasing attack and were short-lived as 'decadence' became specifically associated by the public with the immoral and scandalous conduct of its contributors. Ernest Dowson, Wilde, Max Beerbohm, Lionel Johnson and Aubrey Beardsley were names identified with *The Yellow Book*, founded in 1894. Though the journal was highly popularized by Beardsley's stylized, lewd illustrations, it expelled its artist for personal scandals after the fourth issue. When Symons joined him in founding subsequently *The Savoy* in 1896, the self-appointed historian of decadence had reason fully to dispel the 'yellow' term which was causing so much controversy: 'We are not Realists, or Romanticists, or Decadents. . . . For us all art is good which is good art.'[20]

To what extent the term had indeed become amorphous and nondescript is demonstrated by the gamut of colour symbolism with which it was identified. Next to the *yellow* used to designate the 1890s, the most popular hue was of course the *purple*, the *purple-and-gold* of the dying Roman Empire, appropriated especially in the débâcle of Second-Empire France after the Franco-Prussian War. But there was as well the more subtle white of the lily (expressing the non-involvement and sterility poeticized especially by the Belgian poets of the time[21]), paradoxically called by some the most outrageous. The *green* carnation designated the aesthetes of homosexuality. And Huysmans turned to *orange* as the most sensuous colour in *A Rebours* after describing a decadent feast of *black* foods (with a menu of caviar, olives, turtle soup, black pudding, game in liquorice sauce, chocolates and coffee).

Contemporary with the Aesthetic interpretation, practice and malpractice of decadence were sociological attempts to define the term. The conservative literary and sociological critic, Paul Bourget, was among the most outspoken on the subject. In his *Essais de psychologie contemporaine* (1883 – a date important in terms of convergences of decadent theories), Bourget attributed the term 'decadent' to the collective state of a group of young writers of the 1880s whose excessive individualism entrapped them in an ivory tower.

In fact, incorporated in that volume, though written earlier in 1881, is a section entitled 'Théorie de la décadence' from Bourget's essay on Baudelaire. Not only does he provide a positivistic analysis of decadence, but he looks back to Baudelaire in particular as a decadent prototype, considering a real personality, not a character or a life-style, as representative of a collective psychology. 'Voilà l'homme de la décadence',[22] he says. Bourget's approach is psychological as he detects in Baudelaire's 'Spleen' poems a pathological *ennui* as the crowning symptom of that decadence. Bourget conceives of Baudelaire as having modernized the *tedium vitae* or the secret worm of all declining civilizations, especially that of the previous Latin decadence. Associating Baudelaire distinctly with modern decadence, he goes on to deplore the critical nature of its contemporary manifestation:

> How does it happen that this 'delicate monster' has never more energetically yawned its distress than in the literature of our century in which so many conditions of life are perfectioned, if it is not for the fact that this very perfectioning, in complicating our souls as well, makes us inept for happiness.[23]

Bourget envisaged Baudelaire's decadent modernism and art as by-products of the complexity of his times which he viewed as threatening mankind's capacity for happiness. He associated Baudelaire's poetry broadly with what he considered to be disparate social reactions such as nihilism in Russia, the anarchy of the Commune in France and the philosophical pessimism of Schopenhauer in Germany. With his sociological orientation, he indicts Baudelaire for what he regards as another symptom of decadence: that of inordinate individualism. With his positivistic methodology, he constructs a mechanistic and naturalistic analogy, which demonstrates that excessive egocentrism harms the social mechanism: if a cell should become self-sufficient or irresponsible with respect to a society, the society decomposes:

> If the energy of cells becomes independent, the organisms which comprise the total organism cease similarly to subordinate their individual energy to the total energy, and the anarchy which develops constitutes the decadence of the whole.[24]

This statement concerning the mechanics of social decadence echoes Zola's theory expressed in his *Roman expérimental* of 1880, where he draws a parallel between literary Naturalism and experimental medicine. Later, in 1888, in *The Case of Wagner*, Nietzsche proceeded to attribute the same pattern of decadence to the disturbance he observed in linguistic coherence.

In the case of Bourget, the analogy between social and literary decadence was more explicitly defined:

> The same law governs the development and the decadence of this organism which is language. A decadent style occurs when the unity of the book decomposes to give way to the independence of the page, when the page decomposes to give way to the independence of the sentence, and the sentence to give way to the independence of the word.[25]

He observes the effects of decadence upon literary style as language undergoes a comparable breakdown whereby the whole is expressed through the fragmented parts. As will be seen, Conrad in particular was to make this a premise for his fiction. It is true that Bourget seems to echo Nisard's observations of Latin decadence, but he goes beyond the practices of his contemporary Aesthetes to identify some of the traits which comprise the intrinsic decadence of Zola, Nietzsche and Conrad.

It should be observed, then, that Bourget's is not simply an association of the word decadence with the Art for Art's Sake movement, but a theory establishing decadent style as a literary manifestation of, not escape from, social turmoil. In this respect, Baudelaire serves as a point of departure for this theory, and creates a crossroad between the notion of literary decadence as Aestheticism and the larger context of modern aesthetic Decadence.

While attacking Aestheticism as well as the Naturalists, Max Nordau, the popularizer, journalist and moralist, gives a psychological interpretation of the term 'decadence', literally degenerating it to *Entartung* (1893). He associates the label of 'degeneracy' with a universal fatigue which he perceives as haunting the humanity of his day and pervading late-nineteenth-century writings. In his understanding of the term 'decadent' as simplistically 'immoral', he associates it with some Naturalists such as Zola, whom he berates especially for the blatant exposure of prostitution in *Nana*. (In a self-righteous manner, he decries the French exposure of moral laxity; he adheres to the German cliché of culturally associating the term 'decadent' with the French.) Although his commentary is distinctly non-literary, moralistic and much discredited, it is significant to mention it here, because it does group together such writers as Wilde, Zola and Verlaine, thereby ignoring strict literary boundaries which were being erected between the Aesthetic and Naturalistic schools. Nordau diagnoses the word in terms of a physically and morally contagious mood, characterized by weakness of will, lack of attention and the prevalent feeling of perdition and extinction as a social reality:

> But however silly a term 'fin-de-siècle' may be, the mental constitution which it indicates is actually present in influential circles. The disposition of the times is curiously confused, a compound of feverish restlessness and blunted discouragement, of fearful presage and hang-dog renunciation. The prevalent feeling is that of imminent perdition and extinction. Fin-de-siècle is at once a confession and complaint. The old Northern faith contained the fearsome doctrine of the Dusk of the Gods. In our days there have arisen in more highly developed minds vague qualms of a Dusk of Nations in which all suns and stars are gradually waning . . .[26]

Nordau's 'reportage' of what he regards and foresees as a prevailing mood dissociates the term from the purely artistic focus of the French Symbolists of the 1880s and the English Aesthetes of the 1890s. A Splengerian tone is forecast in his mention of the

Dusk of Nations. It is interesting to note that this later cultural historian of the twentieth century was to delimit 1870 as the beginning of the threat to what he termed as Faustian or Gothic Man's Western European soul.[27]

In the historically self-conscious apprehension of 'decadence', whether in the perception of a Nisard or a Nietzsche, the term did include meanings of both excessive indulgence and oppressive restraint, and as such provides a relevant background for this current study. On the one hand, it designated Latin excesses and Greek over-ripeness coupled with imminent Barbarism in the pivotal state of Byzantium. On the other hand, it alluded to sterile abnegation and passivity, as in Nietzsche's forceful critique of Christianity. Spanning the poles from Pan to Paul, describing both saints and sinners, the word ultimately pointed to conditions which prevented normal functioning, and which led to social and linguistic disequilibrium.

It is to be recognized that those artisans of style who were experimenting with literary expression alone were at the same time self-ordained élites removing themselves from the crisis situations of their societies. They isolated themselves in ivory towers or created for themselves surrogate societies such as fraternities like the Rhymers' Club in England or the coterie group sponsoring Décadisme in France, creating decadent journals in both countries. In their escape into the cult of Aesthetics, they dismissed the everyday and the Philistine for the exceptional and extraordinary. This self-conscious and rebellious Aestheticism has heretofore been most readily associated with the term 'decadence'. Art itself was for them the supreme equivalent of a new hedonistic life-style of sensations and pleasures. As art became the focus and saving grace, the moral tensions in the society producing the revolt of the artists and endemic to the breakdown of previously accepted Western grammars of literary expression, were bracketed by them. In the light of the larger social context, such Aesthetic decadence can be considered as only one particular manifestation of a larger and graver human phenomenon actually expressed and scrutinized in contemporary novels of the late Victorian, Naturalist and Realist schools. For contemporary with *A Rebours* stands Zola's *Germinal* and as notorious as *The Picture of Dorian Gray* is Hardy's *Jude the Obscure*.

The Decadence here described[28] hence surpasses the narrow region of the Aesthetes to encompass an aesthetic, historically delimited, invading the prose medium of key Western European novels of the second half of the nineteenth century which are morally motivated. The following novels are among the best known and provide a cumulative model for the Decadent structure: Dostoevsky's *Idiot*, James's *Ambassadors*, Zola's *Germinal*, Hardy's *Jude the Obscure* and Conrad's *Heart of Darkness*. Such novels explore the repercussions of a divestiture of a tradition of Western moral criteria and of a decline in established religious, aesthetic and philosophical values of the Western world. The authors in the role of observers create a prevailing mood of bleak pessimism in these novels, for they do not prescribe alternatives to the traumas they describe.

Contemporary with the Aesthetes, these writers who grappled with the moral vicissitudes of the second half of the nineteenth century and who were concerned with some form of survival of Western morality unwittingly created a Decadent style. Their moral concern was expressed in their tendency to isolate instances of perversity, paradox and perplexity: conditions which can be considered Decadent because they appear as symptomatic in their writings. They were writers who distilled collective intricacies in individual instances of complexity, making the individual problematic cases into archetypes for a continuous and extended moral trauma. Theirs was not a moralistic condemnation but a human, compassionate sympathy for and empathy with a debilitating and prevailing sense of crisis they observed in their respective societies in transition.

For Decadence implies stalemate and inaction, paralysis as a reaction to moral uncertainty and change, fatigue caused by moral dissolution. The Decadence observed by these authors was not simply the decline of a given value system or a transgression of it. It was the situation where the absence of a coherent value system produced failed individuals suffering from malaise: inactive, incapable of generating progeniture, and unproductive. An aspect of the pessimism of these novels is the lack of competitiveness of the Decadent characters who make no investment in the future. A disintegration of purpose in the characters and of intentionality in the authors is registered.

In the case of poetry, a gradual decline of a signifier, the soul, which I traced in my previous book, *The Symbol of the Soul from Hölderlin to Yeats*,[29] reflected certain moral traumas. Now in the context of the prose of a crisis period in Western literature, the focus is not on the deterioration of a single concept but on the identification of certain symptoms in the narrative, which will be perceived in the successive chapters here contained. In the case of these late nineteenth-century authors, the sense of Decadence is a sensibility betrayed in language, betrayed because the authors themselves transcend the decadence in their achievement of their art, which immunizes them from the unhappy fortunes of their imaginative progeny.

Beyond the particular stylistic signatures of the individual authors in question, there are certain homologous structures in the writing. In the relation between the novels and their social setting, character traits are microstructures of the social shell rather than clearly determined sociological products. There is a collective 'diagnostic' kinship in the grouping of novels as they signal common symptomatic patterns of ineffectuality, self-effacement, non-competitiveness, non-commitment, self-destruction and non-renewal through their characters' passive and solipsistic stances in the setting of prosperous societies – which transcends national barriers.

Eschatological paradigms, to use the critic Frank Kermode's terminology,[30] can be historically located in these late nineteenth-century novels. The characters of the Western Gothic mould are preoccupied consciously or unconsciously with the sense of apocalypse in their extended crisis situations. A clear consciousness of ending in terms of an ending of an era is present, and this literature carries with it an increasing and protracted anticipation.

It is especially interesting to note how certain Decadent patterns recur and are crystallized in the plot, structure, characterization, archetypes, images, vocabulary and tone. It is as if the moral disruption of a society affected the contours of a literary language and structure. Denotative decay is transferred to situations of paradox and the problematic; perversity is the rule rather than the exception, ultimately encoding a Decadent style which will be specifically isolated in the last chapter of this book.

In the context of a philosophical crisis in values, the term 'decadent' is descriptive of the characteristics of a kinship and not as a pejorative or value-charged expression. These writers demonstrate the slippage in the perspective of a set of values which they have not yet relinquished. The word 'decadent', then, is used in this study from the point of view of a socio-aesthetic reading. It is highly identifiable within the major prose narrative of the period prior to the turn of the century. Decadence categorizes a field of transitional literature at the 'midday hour'. It involves a poetics of prose, not poetry. And for this reason, a grammar emerges from its seeds.

2 Dostoevsky and the Gap of Insufficiency

It is paradoxical that, in his effort to create an authentic Christ figure, Dostoevsky produced instead a Decadent archetype in the haunting figure of the Idiot in 1869. His letters are witness to the fact that he toiled with the task of depicting a true Christ or perfect human being. One of the difficulties was that the society in which he lived, he thought, could not lodge such a figure whose model was the Christian diety. He writes of his struggle with 'the idea' of a beautiful individual in a letter to his niece Sofia Alexandrovna in 1868:

> The basic idea is the representation of a truly perfect and noble man. And this is more difficult than anything else in the world, particularly nowadays. All writers, not ours alone but foreigners also, who have sought to represent *Absolute Beauty*, were unequal to the task, for it is an infinitely difficult one. The beautiful is the ideal; but ideals with us as in civilized Europe have long been wavering. There is in the world only one figure of absolute beauty: Christ.[1]

His doubts were indeed justified; for the Idiot character proves both an inadequate re-presentation of the Christ figure and an archetypal challenge to the very conception of Christ which attempts to unite perfection with humanity. Because the Idiot's Christian humanism is at times intemperate and self-motivated, the qualities of mercy, compassion, pity and forgiveness are attenuated and appear out of place in the world surrounding him. The Decadence, hence, is harboured in the gap of insufficiency which makes the 'meek' and innocent Idiot unable to cope with the demands of his surrounding materialistic society. This caesura is highlighted in the 'idiotic' gestures and expression which identify the Idiot and in the epileptic fits which are the

18

symptoms of his malfunctioning. It is heightened by the constant reference to apocalyptic imagery which characters like Lebedev, Ippolit and Rogozhin evoke in conscious interpretation or subconscious dream. In this respect, *The Idiot* is a fountainhead for the thematics of Decadence from the Dostoevsky canon, conceived in the context of individual destiny. Dostoevsky posits an ideal only to approximate it, and in enacting an insufficient imitation, he creates an aesthetics of Decadence in that discrepancy.

Whereas decadence is generally associated with immorality and corruption, that which Dostoevsky boldly paints all over his fiction as a 'given', in this novel it becomes identified with passive goodness and meekness as expressions of insufficiency. This represents a reversal of the conventional definition of the term. For it is not in the vile figures that Dostoevsky perceives the decadence, but rather in the Christianly charitable ones who avoid commitment. Dostoevsky insists on the failure of Christianity to withstand the challenges of evolving industrialism and socialism so rampant in his era. And he demonstrates, particularly in the Idiot character, how the Christian falls painfully short of fulfilling his humanistic purposes. The point is not that the Idiot is too Christian but rather that he is not Christian enough and does not, in effect, live up to the Christ model of functioning within the world. Excessive pride and self-involvement weaken his responsiveness to his environment. In some respects, he is like the Greek figure of innocence, Hippolytus, who taints his unequalled innocence, with pride, and thereby ironically destroys its salutary effects. Beyond the casting of double and meek types, so often viewed as Dostoevsky's unique contribution to fiction, is this identification of a Christian Decadent type which becomes a personification of a failure in terms of a religious culture.

It is significant to observe that Dostoevsky uses an epithet 'idiot' whose root meaning derives from the Western Greek context. *Idiotes* designated a private person as opposed to one holding a public office. It came to mean a man who did not go into the market place, someone who differed from everyone else, someone on his own. Beyond the religious context to which Dostoevsky applied it, it represents a case of extreme individualism and as such incurs a cultural connotation of the individualistic type in the Western heritage. The most comprehensive implication of the term is that of incompleteness which typified both the principal character and the structure of this architectonic novel.

The Idiot is not only puzzling, but is a puzzle with cracks in its make-up. He is the first of a set of ambiguous characters or conundrums which will be identified in Decadent fiction. He was considered by his author as 'sphinx-like', and appropriately so, as he appears often immobile and impenetrable. In the course of the novel, those cracks become more clearly viewed as defects, and in the critical incident when he breaks the fragile vase in the presence of the nobility, he becomes identified as a 'defective' prince.

As will be seen in the case of Henry James as well, the Decadent is ultimately the missing element which cannot be expressed but which is more present than that which is apparent. Dostoevsky's novel traces the process whereby the ideal desists from becoming real and incarnated, and is relegated instead to the region of the inarticulate. The fact that this Christ figure is not accepted by the given society is due in part to the ineffective way by which he expresses his values. The entire work produces the stylistic effect of insubstantiality and deficiency. It suggests an absence of something prodigious.

A general disorientation is established at the beginning of the novel when it is learned that the Idiot, Prince Myshkin, a young man aged 27, an impoverished noble, had been estranged from his native Russia for a period of four years. Having been retained in a sanatorium in Switzerland for his epileptic condition, he is about to return to his native soil. It becomes clear, however, that this physical disorientation is not the major cause of his awkwardness, and that the estrangement is more metaphysical than social or temporal. For at the end of the novel the Idiot is even further removed from his society and his condition of isolation and dislocation is aggravated even as he re-establishes links with relatives within the upper crust of the society. Ironically, any trace of a *Bildungsroman* is avoided as the character returns to Switzerland in a worsened epileptic condition and is marked by a naïveté which has become an inanity. In this primary, skeletal scheme, a general pattern of decline is traced and accentuated by a series of catastrophes which involve the consumptive Ippolit, Nastasya who is murdered, Rogozhin's insanity and Aglaya's mismarriage and departure from Russia.

The manifestations of the Idiot's failure recur in myriad instances throughout the novel, highlighting the character's momentary disorientations and general inadaptability to the *milieu* and the *moment*. The first demonstration of his ineffectuality occurs when he is introduced into the Ivolgin household and finds himself in the midst of a verbal dispute between Ganya and Varya over Nastasya, the 'fallen' woman. Varya is anxiously attempting to prevent a possible liaison of her brother with Nastasya, fearing the further defamation of her degenerating family, whose head is the drunken, former army officer, the General Ivolgin. The Prince finds himself inadvertently positioned between the two combatants and receives the slap which Ganya had intended to inflict upon his sister. Instead of retaliating or reacting emotionally, the Prince emits a strange, incongruous smile which becomes a sign of his idiocy:

> Exclamations could be heard on all sides. The prince turned pale. He looked Ganya straight in the face with strange, reproachful eyes; his lips quivered as he tried to say something; they were twisted into a strange and completely incongruous smile.[2]

This response is strikingly unsuitable and inappropriate and is regarded as such by the band of operators and usurers who witness it. It also serves to debase him in the eyes of the nobility who learn of it. It seems to initiate a series of symbolic self-effacements which the Idiot undergoes in the novel.

As the critical moments multiply, the placidity of the Prince becomes increasingly disturbing to the other characters and subsequently to the reader. When Rogozhin, the rich merchant and surrogate 'brother' of Myshkin, attempts to kill him in the corridor of his lodging, Myshkin readily forgives him and continues to regard him as his friend. When Nastasya withdraws from Myshkin in the marriage ceremony and makes a fool of him, Myshkin fails to fight for what was a commitment to him. These passive stances *vis-à-vis* the crucial prerogatives of life and love are increasingly associated with the Idiot figure. This passive quality becomes symptomatic of an ellipsis in Myshkin's behaviour. The principle of 'Christian self-denial', to use a term employed by the philosopher J. S. Mill and pertinent also to Thomas Hardy, appears to be undermined through Myshkin's case. For the Idiot, in continuously allowing himself to be humiliated by one blow after another, removes himself from the struggle for survival around him, and is thereby responsible for his own devaluation within his society. Far from commending him for such restraint or self-sacrifice, his society stigmatizes him with the label of idiocy. A general dearth of energy, a lethargy, characterizes the Idiot figure. As if lacking in vital breath, listlessly he proceeds in his human dealings. In addition, at times his position is one of entrapment as he seems to be victimized by the combination of his character and the circumstance and consequently is caught in a posture of inaction which foretells his doom. In situations that require action on his part, the Prince stalls and resists active engagement. The instances are many, but include Rogozhin's challenge of rivalry for the hand of Nastasya. In the scene in Part Two when Myshkin visits Rogozhin's house, he fails actively to generate the jealousy he might naturally harbour for Nastasya. This lack of appropriate signalling and avowal, this hesitancy to move toward commitment of feeling and subsequent action, weaken Myshkin's position with respect to his rival, Rogozhin. While Myshkin abounds in compassion for his fellow man, he lacks the fervour of passion and the sexual drive. This is especially demonstrated in the relationships he has with the contrasting females, Nastasya and Aglaya.

His equivocal attitude toward these two women disables him from having a fulfilling relationship with either one of them. He is simultaneously attracted to the morally loose woman of gentry origin and the bourgeois virgin of the established Russian society, and he vacillates between these two poles. His detached position in his pity for the fallen Nastasya and his esteem for the reputable Aglaya precludes a possessiveness which an amorous relationship would require. Nastasya is a complex mystery for him to probe, representing a worldliness which is attractive and novel, and he is obsessively haunted by the abstract idea of her rather than her person. He pities her and views her slippage from the landed gentry as a sociological phenomenon, as a symbol of St Petersburg in decay. But his failure to experience a real sexual drive for her is shown in the contrast with Rogozhin, who regards her as a sexual object to be possessed, conquered and consumed. Aglaya, on the other hand, the model specimen of the upper middle crust, represents bourgeois values to which he is drawn in his desire to reintegrate with his society and country. But it becomes obvious that he would be incapable of assuming a position of responsibility which a commitment to her would entail.

In a climactic but symptomatic scene the Idiot, faced with the final choice between the two women, stalls. It is ironically this inaction which determines the choice rather than a willed and conscious decision. In this instance, Myshkin's gap of insufficiency is demonstrated in his failure in verbal expression. At consequential moments when verbal power could serve as a means for acquisition and assertiveness, the Idiot remains stunned and dumbstruck. This is the case when the exasperated Aglaya challenges him to an outright public declaration of love. Myshkin fails to respond to the cue at the appropriate moment and is inarticulate. As Aglaya rushes out, interpreting this as a rejection, the Idiot passively accepts the substitute of Nastasya, who falls unconscious in his arms, overcome by the dramatics of the scene. The Prince's verbal paralysis blocks the emergence and cultivation of feeling. His emotional integrity is threatened by a diffusion of exposures and continuous interruption – a phenomenon which will be equally observed in the cases of James and Hardy.

The impartial observer, Radomsky, often regarded as conveying Dostoevsky's own voice, comments on the Prince's sudden abandonment of Aglaya, and diagnoses the Idiot's failing as an incapacity to love: 'No, Prince, she won't understand! Aglaya loved like a woman, like a human being, and not like – a disembodied spirit! Do you know what I think, my poor Prince? Most likely you've never loved either of them!' (627). This is in response to the Prince's statement that he loved both women. Radomsky's implication is that the Prince is insufficiently carnal. By calling him a 'disembodied spirit', he implies that the Prince is asexual. He recognizes how abstract the Prince is. Once again, this might be reflecting Dostoevsky's aesthetic position regarding his Decadent persona, for in depicting the decline of a type, he had to remain on the level of abstraction.

Not only is the Prince reticent in his self-expression, but when he does use language, he misuses it. This is particularly apparent in the birthday party scene early in the novel when a number of suitors are bidding competitively for Nastasya's hand in marriage. In his own marriage proposal to Nastasya, momentarily drawn as he is into the general activity, the Prince considers that her consent would be an 'honour' and he publicly declares his 'respect' for her. This inappropriate language with respect to the Nastasya character prompts the company to designate him as an idiot. It also fails to capture Nastasya, who abandons him to spend the night with Rogozhin. The society's perception of him as innocent works against him since that is a value which it has rejected. Myshkin's failure to communicate his meaning effectively in such instances widens the lacuna between himself and his society, and in this way the Idiot can be identified with the root meaning of the word. The recurring blankness of the Idiot's verbal and facial expression at crucial moments of reckoning is a blatant sign of his idiocy. It also identifies him as a child, for often in his efforts towards sincerity, he defies social conventions.

Myshkin's aloofness or neglect of the mechanism of his society is not, however, simply due to inherent naïveté. His singular posture is caused rather by his aristocratic pride and egotistical propensity. At times he avoids succumbing to human contact and hence refrains from becoming fully involved with others. He accentuates his individuality to an extreme without making himself a viable component of his society. Disdaining what he sees before him as mankind, he isolates himself in a superior position. There are indeed ironic overtones to the statement that Nastasya makes – calling him the only *real person* she has seen. For, paradoxical as it may seem, the Idiot is more substantial than the traces of men before him. The irony is that the 'reality' to which Nastasya is referring has become regarded as obsolete. Belonging to a previous value system, he possesses a character that can have a defect or be tragic. The others around him are too diffuse ever to be considered defective.

But in remaining innocent to the realm of actual realistic experience because of his distaste for it, he is increasingly gullible to deception and discredits himself, thereby catalyzing his own demise. The Prince's knowledge of evil is vicarious, often relegated to the subconscious realm of *alter ego* figures such as Rogozhin. He is oblivious to the way evil functions. The Burdovsky affair demonstrates how blind the Prince is to the conspiring and corrupt forces of his 'flabby' society. There could be no better example of the debilitating effects of such innocence than in the key incident when Myshkin loses his inheritance to a group of extortioners. He allows his birthright, what would indeed make him respectable in his society, to slip away from him, to be devoured by the adventurers and fortune-seekers. The recognition of that atmosphere of social decadence, to which the Prince remains obstinately impervious, is articulated by Kolya Ivolgin, who describes the spirit of the times:

There are very few honest people here, so few that there is nobody one can entirely respect. . . . And have you noticed, Prince, that in our age everyone is a sordid adventurer! And that is particularly true of Russia, of our dear motherland. And how it all happened, I don't understand. Everything seemed to be built on such solid foundations, but what is it like now? Everyone is talking about it. Everywhere they are writing about it. (164)

The impersonal 'it' in reference to the decadence of the times emphasizes the self-consciousness of the social state. It becomes atmospheric like a moral disease and is communicated as a condition. Dostoevsky, like the other authors here examined, depicts the environment as a living organism with which the individual has to contend. This comes close to the volatile climate which Zola also paints in his frescoes of Second Empire France, undergoing comparable changes and ferment.

By losing his inheritance, the Prince is confirmed as a devalued object in a fallen world. His mission as an ardent Slavophile promoting Russian Orthodox Messianism seems merely nominal as is highlighted by the maladroitness with which he addresses that cause at the Yepanchin engagement party. He seems to lack intention and purpose as he wanders through the novel and ironically only succeeds in undermining his own reputation in all circles. Hence, his breaking of the Chinese vase after his inappropriate tirade seems inevitable as foreseen by Aglaya Yepanchin. The ensuing epileptic attack dramatically underlines his ineptness. The broken vase, comparable in impact to the inappropriate smile, becomes the objective correlative of the defective condition of the Decadent archetype: the beautiful object, cracked and flawed.

Whereas on the surface, in a Naturalistic novel, the society would be assumed to be the decadent factor, in this work Dostoevsky poses the pendulent problematic of two extremes – that is, the decadence of the society and the more succinct one of character. This gives decadence a broader base, the one more subtle than the other. The perverse alteration of connotation turns a meaning against itself and gives it a pejorative sense. The compounded Decadence creates a situation in which the very forces which might have struggled against it are caught in an impasse and inaction. It confronts a moral impotence with a moral degradation. The Idiot 'situation' with respect to the world thereby coalesces the two facets of Decadence – based on excess.[3]

An essential *missing* ingredient in the Idiot's make-up, as Dostoevsky himself attested in his telling letter to his niece, is the comic sense:

> of all the noble figures in Christian literature, I reckon Don Quixote as the most perfect. But Don Quixote is noble only by being at the same time comic. The reader feels sympathy and compassion with the Beautiful, derided and unconscious of its own worth.[4]

It is significant that Dostoevsky chooses the *Quixote* as harbouring his model for human perfection, for in that novel the tension between the real and the ideal was alleviated by an author who reconciled the two by comic reservation. It is paradoxically the comic incredibility of the 'ideal' character that makes it viable. Because he does not approach his character seriously, because he does not deal with it ontologically, the author can let his character survive endlessly. In marvelling at the discrepancy between the real and the ideal, he is free to firmly posit the ideal on realistic soil. Once the ideal gives up its claim to reality, and is distanced by satire, it functions unself-consciously, uninhibited, on realistic terrain, negating itself while robustly manifesting itself in the flesh.

That the two works are compared is appropriate in that they both can be regarded as transitional. Both characters bring to their worlds inappropriate, outdated codes and conventions and are recognized as ludicrous. In the case of *Don Quixote*, it is the question of the chivalric code; in the case of *The Idiot*, it is the more generalized Christian one. In both instances, the heroes behave according to conventions whose values have been lost. The knight and the Christ figure are two devalued specimens in their respective worlds, which are in the process of transition. But the similarity stops here for the very reason that the *Quixote* becomes a comic work and *The Idiot* a Decadent one. As Dostoevsky himself realized, Cervantes succeeded in what he could not do. The comic ingredient provided by the Sancho Panza character in that novel anchors the ideal to realistic grounds. Panza does not undermine Quixote but completes him, and in this respect provides for the humanization of the ideal. Quixote's lack of self-consciousness is disarming, and it is that which draws the reader to him. With a willing suspension of disbelief the reader endorses what he may intellectually regard as untenable and outmoded values. As Dostoevsky remarked, one feels sympathy for the character and responds emotionally to his generous, outgoing qualities. The 'seduction' by the ideal character has taken place through the emotional gateway.

Because of his comic deficiency, Myshkin lacks the charm, charisma and generosity to render his humanism effective. He lacks the comic armour necessary to withstand the absurdist tendencies around him. As will be seen, there is a tendency in Decadent narrative to render the chief figure all too spiritual and abstract. As Rogozhin notes, Myshkin is 'not all there'. He belongs to the other world of saints and demons and, as such, is inaccessible and distant.

The Idiot's cool rationalism makes him unable to enjoy life nor fully participate in it. Lebedev remarks how little the Idiot knows life. The cynical jesting of Lebedev is completely foreign to him. The earthiness of many of the characters is alien to him. This parsiminous attitude toward life, this rational circumvention of it, is a Decadent trait identified with the Idiot and to be seen simultaneously in the chief figures of Henry James and Thomas Hardy. It can be identified as the element of the pristine. It can also be viewed as the primal ingredient of the Decadent factor which operates against the life principle.

Eschatological commentary and imagery overshadow the focal point of the Idiot figure; they are used aesthetically in the novel and are expressed through dream, nightmare, hallucination, confession and pictoral art. Four key references to the Apocalypse itself appear and contribute to the eschatological backdrop. The two underworld figures who surround the Idiot, Lebedev and Ippolit, are haunted by the Apocalypse and attempt interpretations of it. Rogozhin seems to incarnate the Apocalyptic beast. These figures convey an irrationality expressed through ironic buffoonery or mad anguish which undermine the earnestness of the Idiot figure and belie the sincerity of his expression.

Central to the novel is the Hans Holbein painting of *Christ Taken from the Cross*, harboured as it is within the gloomy house of Rogozhin. It was precisely this image of the dead Christ, captured in the painting, that had been the germ for *The Idiot*. Having seen the original in Basle, the impressionable novelist was obsessed by it, and proceeded to construct the novel around such an aesthetic document. He strategically placed a reproduction of this Western art product within the house of Rogozhin. The Idiot himself is the first to comment on it, saying that the suffering therein displayed could cause one to lose faith. The portrait strikes him all too intimately, as if he identifies with it as an objectification of his own demise.

This isolated view of the crucifixion represented by the portrait becomes a Decadent image, for it suggests only part of the whole Christ scheme particularly from the vantage point of the Russian Orthodox Church, which attached more significance to the Resurrection than to the Crucifixion. Accordingly, Rogozhin's perspective is incomplete and partial, a metonymy of the whole, and is readily associated with disbelief. Isolated as the portrait is, it conveys a fragment which can be considered Decadent. It represents the decomposition and weakening which Dostoevsky begins to identify distinctly with the Western context of Christianity.

What makes this portrait of Christ vividly Decadent is the illusion it gives of a naturalistic portrayal. It focuses on the realistic rendering of Christ rather than on an allegorical one. It is thereby associated with the destructive forces, rational in origin, which Dostoevsky considered as Western cultural influence, and shunned. The Christ figure in the painting is carnal and his mortal wounds are highlighted in painful misery. There, all the mystery of the Christ figure is foresaken as it is drawn within the context of his humanity rather than his divinity, and mortality is transfixed in the lethal expression of the dead man's vacant and glassy eyes:

> In the picture the face is terribly smashed with blows, swollen, covered with terrible, swollen and blood stained bruises, the eyes open and squinting; the large, open whites of the eyes have a sort of dead and glassy glint. (447)

The portrait remains a startling image of death, eliminating the transcendent aspect from the Christ figure. It seems to support precisely Dostoevsky's fears of humanizing Christ.

Such an image is, instead, a challenge to the Christ figure and becomes identified by Ippolit as the Antichrist. The dying consumptive Ippolit, the living emblem of death who also haunts the Idiot as a frail shadow, interprets the picture in his 'essential explanation' of the Apocalypse:

> Looking at that picture you get the impression of nature as some enormous, implacable and dumb beast, or to put it more correctly, much more correctly, though it may seem strange, as some huge engine of the latest design which has senselessly seized, cut to pieces, and swallowed up – impassively and unfeelingly – a great and priceless Being. (447)

The notion of the Apocalyptic beast is introduced in the subsequent image of the tarantula which Ippolit recalls from a nightmare vision as suggestive of the biblical serpent or satanic demon whose reign spans the period of the Antichrist. Through Ippolit's vision, Dostoevsky imagines the rare and precious being of Christ in jeopardy. Like Zola and Conrad after him, he uses a mechanistic metaphor to depict the consumptive aspect of a society out to destroy the human element.

By the power of association, the images of the Antichrist are identified with the character of Rogozhin, who is the object of Ippolit's hallucination. It becomes apparent that Rogozhin incarnates the bestial power, emerging as he does impetuously from dark corridors and dwellings. The death gaze of the portrait resembles the sexual look of Rogozhin's expressionistic eyes. As a character, Rogozhin threatens the Idiot. There is the actual instance when he nearly attacks him with a knife in a corridor. The Idiot is tormented by Rogozhin's eyes, which perpetually haunt him and lead him to states of apocalyptic insight comparable in intensity with St John's.

Rogozhin's affair with Nastasya reflects very closely the biblical archetype of the Apocalyptic beast and its harlot. Together they enact the paradigm of the Antichrist in the vicinity of the Idiot. One has only to recall the scriptural imagery of the whore of Babylon, holding the cup of abominations as she rides the imperial beast or symbol of 'decadent' Rome, to associate this with Nastasya and her situation in St Petersburg. Rogozhin and Nastasya become inseparable despite the many attempts to sever their relationship. They face the Idiot with implications of death, sexuality and instinct. And the Idiot is witness to that bestial force which eventually kills the Harlot in his midst, at the close of the novel.

It is the shadowy Ippolit, on the verge of death, who is the major vehicle transmitting the Apocalyptic vision from his dreams and hallucinations through his public testimony or 'essential explanation'. Like the author, Dostoevsky himself, he remarks how he was haunted all his life by an idea which failed to emerge totally. He expresses Dostoevsky's own bout with the Ideal and Decadence which does not allow that Ideal to be expressed. The aesthetic goal hence becomes associated with an eschatological paradigm representing the void created by the excesses of a materialistic society:

> in every idea of genius or in every new human idea, or, more simply still, in every serious human idea born in anyone's brain, there is something that cannot possibly be conveyed to others, though you wrote volumes about it and spent thirty-five years in explaining your idea; something will always be left that will obstinately refuse to emerge from your head and that will remain with you forever; and you will die without having conveyed to anyone what is perhaps the most vital point of your idea. (433)

The 'explanation' of this gap in expression is found in the forces of the Antichrist which undermine the Idiot.

The Idiot later provides further explanation for his own incompetence when he refers to the diffusiveness of the individual in the modern world[5] – a condition which prevents modern man from being the complete human being of earlier times. He implies that previously man was more complete: modern man has no focus, is broadened and wider, compelled by multiple ideas and visions. The type of individual of which the Idiot is an imitation is no longer viable. In the novel, Dostoevsky enacts the diffusion of that central character. Structurally, the novel represents a mirage of disparate segments without a binding idea.

The third character to foreshadow the Idiot through apocalyptic connotations is Lebedev. He joins the cast of fainter and lesser personages that undermine the integrity of the central character. While Ippolit makes an existential reference to the Apocalypse, the lowly Lebedev evokes Apocalyptic imagery through ironic commentary: he becomes known as one who makes a hobby of interpreting the Apocalypse. With an attitude of jest and buffoonery, he assumes a philosophic stance, diagnosing his age as the era of the Antichrist. He alludes to the image of the third horse, the biblical emblem and sign of moral turpitude in a society grown flabby and weak:

> we've arrived at the time of the third horse, the black one, and of the rider who has a pair of balances in his hand, for everything in our present age is weighed in the scales and everything is settled by agreement and all people are merely seeking their rights. 'A measure of wheat for a penny, and three measures of barley for a penny.' (232)

Barter and usury which characterize this category are vividly demonstrated in the dealings of the society which surrounds the Idiot, from Ganya's mercenary ambitions to the underworld figures who succeed in depriving the Idiot of his lawful fortune. Lebedev also makes mention of the wormwood which in the original biblical connotation is a falling star that polluted the waters. In the context of *The Idiot*, it relates to widespread corruption of commerce and inordinate materialism which are shown to have infected the terrain. In its meaning as a bitter plant, this image of an unpleasant association reflects the spiritual aridity of a society which creates figures like Lebedev who crawl on blighted surfaces.

Not only does Lebedev comment on the times, but he impersonates them as well. A Judas-like figure, he eventually betrays the Idiot in the Burdovsky affair. He supplies facts for the libellous newspaper article which falsifies Myshkin's position. He is thus instrumental in supplanting Myshkin by Burdovsky, depriving Myshkin of the inheritance he was to get from his benefactor. Lebedev also intrudes in the correspondence between Aglaya and Nastasya, which serves to spoil the Prince's reputation. Lebedev perpetrates 'the lie' but paradoxically his interpretations bear trappings of 'higher truths'. His hypocrisy is a foil to Myshkin's literal sincerity, his mockery, a defamation of the redemptive beauty which the Prince extols.

Lebedev's anti-heroic stances and ironic posture undermine the passive heroics of the Prince in a manner resembling that of a Shakespearean fool. Odious and animal-like in association, he walks a tightrope of incredulity, witnessing the slow and self-defeating progress of the Prince and steadily contributing to that demise. He also seems to be like Nietzsche's fool in *Thus Spoke*

Zarathustra, who pushes the last man off the tightrope into an abyss. In the struggle of good and evil, Lebedev incarnates that which is vile – and is aware of it: 'I am vile, vile, I feel it.' (271) He suggests morphologically a subtle assailant of the virtuous. His tone approximates the Zarathustra-like challenge to Christian piety and authenticity. His language, replete with irony, is a deceitful and stylized form of expression. Whereas the Prince fails in expression and cannot handle irony himself, Lebedev perversely excels in interpretation and becomes the spokesman, both in style and comment, of the spirit of the times.

And so, the characters in *The Idiot* are poetically conceived, known through their gestures and gait, identified by their discourse rather than through a prosaically determined psychology. Their significance is figurative, as they become mythical in representation and are recognizable in outline and energy, much like the dying figures or shadows which the poet William Butler Yeats was later to envision as having decadent associations. Yeats's expression, 'the autumn of the body', borrowed from the essay of that title, best describes this poetic tenor of character which has been suggested in *The Idiot*:

> I see, indeed, in the arts of every country those faint lights and faint colours and faint outlines and faint energies which many call 'the decadence', and which I, because I believe that the arts lie dreaming of things to come, prefer to call the autumn of the body.[6]

In this perspective, Rogozhin is a drive, slicing like a knife throughout a dark world. Lebedev is an earthly slug, crawling on terrain. Ippolit is a skeleton, unsubstantial, a disembodied voice. Nastasya is a corpse of beauty. Finally Myshkin is an expression, and the gap in his character is represented by that strange contortion of smile which reflects an innate shyness and inadequacy. This pageant of figures enacts an eschatological pattern, both thematically and stylistically. It has a cumulative effect of undermining the notion of an integrated character in the narrative. Dostoevsky has here diffused character into forms and forces interacting with each other in a drama of attrition. He has substituted for the realistic presentation of character a mythic and symbolic one.

The polyphony of voices, expressed by Lebedev, Ippolit and

Rogozhin counter the inarticulate, silent state of Myshkin. The insufficiency in Myshkin's character is conveyed most forcefully through this gap in his expression. His failure to communicate effectively makes him fail in one of the chief responsibilities of the humanist. As seen, the effect he perpetrates is one of chronic blockage. He is incapable of fulfilling himself in either personal relationships or public mission. Whereas on the one hand, the suffering of the Idiot figure who fails in his goodness against the forces of evil would make of him a Christ figure, the other aspect of Christ, the thrust toward moral progress, is missing. It is because of this lack that the messianic Christ archetype is transformed into one of decadence. Having pursued a course of withdrawal from society rather than active participation and involvement, he assumes the root meaning of the word Idiot. His proceedings persistently fall short of completion.

The religious crisis poetically conceived in *The Idiot* is prosaically debated in the dialects of *The Brothers Karamazov* (1880) and in its immoral universe. There the emphasis is less upon the maladjustments or individual inadequacies of a Christ figure than upon possible alternatives to a Myshkin débâcle, shifting the emphasis from individual suffering and trauma to collective responsibility. As Dostoevsky seems to have resolved some of his religious and ideological uncertainties, his later novel reverts to a more traditional and realistic form and loses the signs of Decadence.

It is a significant biographical fact that Dostoevsky wrote *The Idiot* abroad during a period (1867–71) in which he still harboured his youthful doubts about the Christian religion – prior to his return to Russia and the Orthodox Church in 1871. He can be biographically identified with his principal character in that both were estranged from their country and under Western influence. In many ways, Dostoevsky shared in the ideological turmoil of the times, in the crisis of faith which Matthew Arnold had notably expressed in his poem 'Dover Beach' in 1867. The lines are worth repeating here:

> The Sea of Faith
> Was once, too, at the full, and round earth's shore
> Lay like the folds of a bright girdle furl'd.
> But now I only hear
> Its melancholy, long, withdrawing roar,

Retreating . . :
And we are here as on a darkling plain
Swept with confused alarms of struggle and flight,
Where ignorant armies clash by night.

Dostoevsky's attitude toward Christianity in that early period is Western in orientation, and he casts characters which reflect the fragmentation and challenge, creating an aesthetic from that perturbed sensibility. Characteristically, the scrutiny is upon individual destiny in *The Idiot*. It is particularly interesting that Dostoevsky develops the kind of fiction which is here viewed as Decadent at a time when he was most closely exposed to the West – reflecting both a personal and a collective crisis.

Simultaneously, as many critics have noted, his own ideological definition of decadence also begins to emerge. It refers specifically to the corruption that Roman Catholicism represented to him and the Utopian theories rampant in Western Europe stemming as he saw it from individualistic ideology. Dostoevsky was establishing broad analogies between socialism, atheism, Catholicism and materialism. And *The Idiot* contains this atavistic attitude, particularly in the fact that Aglaya Yepanchin 'succumbs' to a 'decadent' marriage with a phony Polish count and to prospects of migration to the West.

From this vantage point, Soviet critics have regarded Dostoevsky's work as 'decadent' in Marxist thematology. It is true that *The Idiot* is a prognosis of a recognized faltering condition: Dostoevsky was to observe subsequently at the time of the Paris Commune in 1871 that, in losing Christ, the West was collapsing.[7] But the attempt at prescription in *The Brothers Karamazov* seems outside the guidelines of Marxist doctrine. The critic René Fuelop-Muller has recognized the ethical disparity between Dostoevsky and his socialist contemporaries. Inevitably, Dostoevsky returns to a reassessment of the Christ figure as the only means of restoring individual dignity within a context of the collectivism of Eastern Orthodoxy. Konstantin Mochulsky's view of the author as insistently Christian becomes justified in the context of Dostoevsky's later novel. The Decadence here detected occurs when Dostoevsky does not have the support of an ideological religiosity.

In *The Brothers Karamazov*, the trauma of the gap is removed as Dostoevsky returns to a more fully integrated Christ figure in the person of Aloysha. It is precisely because the centrality of a meek figure is dispelled that there is no threat to it. In focusing upon the collective identity and responsibility of a family, the notion of an imperilled individual identity is lost. Some critics have schematized that composite whole into the elements of intellect (Ivan), senses (Dimitri) and spirit (Aloysha). Here Aloysha does not confront a metaphorical brother as does Myshkin, but two real ones. He does not observe the drama but in fact participates in it and shares the burden of patricide. The vital sensual forces apparent in that family unit contribute to the strengthening of the Christian figure rather than to its weakening. The work is oriented toward a messianic, future-oriented post-lapsarian perspective rather than derived from a pre-lapsarian one of regret and decline.

A healthy fortitude, not a weakness, marks Aloysha's attitude toward the realm of experience, as he becomes combative with a much more ardent, less disinterested form of compassion (than in the case of the Idiot) which he extends to Lise and his negating kin. Rather than being isolated and confined to a monastary, Aloysha is urged by the wise Father Zossima to relate to the crowd and to marry. Aloysha connects with the world. And at his moment of mystic revelation he sensually touches the earth in a tangible form of ecstasy: a symbolic gesture of that integration.

In this context, the schematic dialectics so pervasive in *The Brothers Karamazov*, often on the subject of the Antichrist in the studied dialogues that Ivan has, for example, with Aloysha, replace the more subtle and symbolic juxtapositions of figures and apocalyptic paradigms in *The Idiot*. In the later more conventional novel, the personalities are more firmly delimited and materially based. They do not elude the reader; they are consistent with Dostoevsky's firmer commitment to the Eastern Christian doctrine. It is as if he finally arrived at an orthodox creed of communality as an answer to the traumatic atrophy and debilitating isolation that he had experienced in Western individualism. *The Brothers Karamazov* offers a distinct contrast to the arena of nebulous forces contending with each other in *The Idiot*. For in the latter, less articulated identities grope in an atmosphere of moral ambiguity and illustrate what Ippolit had diagnosed as the diffusiveness of modern man.

It is interesting and worth noting that Nietzsche's *Antichrist* (1888) is written after *The Idiot* and that the philosopher in fact mentions the Russian writer as having influenced his version of the Antichrist. Nietzsche actually uses the word 'Idiotum' to label the humble types esteemed in Christian doctrine: 'That queer and sick world into which the Gospels introduce us, as in a Russian novel, a world in which the scum of society, nervous disorders, and childlike idiocy [*kindliches Idiotum*] seem to be having a rendezvous.'[8] He proceeds to identify the ecstatic states of the religious man as a sick and epileptoid form. He mockingly views the Christian archetype of perfection as the 'pale, sickly, *idiotic* enthusiastic character'[9] (emphasis added). And he inevitably associated the word 'decadent' with this type while attesting to Dostoevsky's empathy with it: 'It is regrettable that a Dostoevsky did not live near this most interesting of all decadents. I mean someone who would have known how to sense the very stirring charm of such a mixture of the sublime, the sickly and childlike.'[10]

It has been seen how, at a momentous point, Dostoevsky *did* identify the perplexity of such an admixture, and created in form and character a lingering Decadent anomaly. *The Idiot* proves paradoxical in the Decadence it conveys, for the author is both asserting the Christ figure and demonstrating its inviability. The novel diffuses and destroys its original model through the structural accumulation of recurring gaps expressed in terms of insufficiency of momentum, weakness of breath, cracks in the surface. This is attested to in the constant preoccupation in the novel with the 'idea' which fails to emerge and the tedious approximation of it. Dostoevsky creates a model of decline in this waning of an archetype precious to Western fiction. It is a model appropriated in different ways by his contemporaries, James, Hardy, Zola and Conrad, as they proceed to encode further features of the Decadent.

3 Henry James and the Poetics of Postponement

To associate Henry James with a 'decadent' rubric could appear inappropriate in view of his moral imperative, derived as it was from Puritan New England. For in his literary criticism, James rallied against those European authors who exhibited the obvious signs of moral weakness, criticizing, for example, Flaubert's *Madame Bovary* for its concern with the 'paltry' and its exposure of moral turpitude. And in his treatment of the international theme in his novels, this author who eventually forsook his American nationality for British citizenship continued to identify moral corruption with the Europeans. To them he exposed his 'naïve' Americans. His well-known short story *Daisy Miller* (1878) is the most obvious example of the kind of stereotype he perpetuated: the innocent American girl named after an uncultivated field flower (rather than the hothouse flowers of the Symbolists or the jaded orchids of the Aesthetes) being destroyed by the 'Roman Fever' representing a cultural sense of European decay.

The more elaborate juxtaposition of the American unspoiled persona with the European decadent stereotypes is exemplified simultaneously in James's longer narrative, *The American* (1877). There, what characterizes the American *vis-à-vis* the Europeans is his energy and decisiveness as opposed to the lack of such qualities in the European aristocrats desperately maintaining their *status quo*. With the focus of this novel on cultural clashes and misunderstandings, such confrontations begin to be encoded in a stylistic expression of Decadence. Marriage as a device for dénouement is absent in his novel, leaving an ambiguous ending which was to become a typical Jamesian pattern. More importantly, this novel marks the beginning of a series of portrayals that demonstrate a contamination of the American types as they begin to fail in their notable quality of decision-making, intention and resolution.

In James's fiction, the single trait which identifies in his prose style the expression of Decadence is that of postponement. In almost all his tales and novels the protaganists, both American and European, are debilitated by a chronic tendency to postpone and avoid. This stylistic element becomes a reflection of a certain inadequacy they all share in life situations. It is the germ of a Decadent *écriture* which James originates as a critic of his time, and it affects the very structure of his novels in terms of plot, crisis and ending. Whether or not its psychological aspect reflects James's own personal attitude as an observer of life is a biographical question. Beyond reflecting any individual idiosyncrasy, this style draws James into a larger context of European authors who portray common symptomatic patterns within a common climate.

In such works as *The American*, *The Portrait of a Lady* (1881) and *The Ambassadors* (1903), the postponement of action is evidenced in the behaviour of the characters and in the unfurling of the plot. This static character seen in James becomes a significant feature of the modern problematic of atrophy. The hesitancy toward commitment, the failure in decision-making, the breakdown in communication and the weakening of passion result in cases of psychological and social ineffectuality. The emphasis upon the missed experience and hence the inarticulate are the ultimate outcome of these perverse strides of postponement in James's major characters. A continuous stance of *waiting* characterizes their behaviour, and often the attention is more on what is not said than on what is said. This aspect of James's prose was to be stylized in works of his later period, beginning with *The Golden Bowl* (1904), turgid with linguistic play.

The allegorical form of this Decadence is most obvious in the masterful short story 'The Beast in the Jungle'. It describes a man who is waiting for something to happen and has lost life in the process. It presents the typical Jamesian persona, the procrastinator who postpones life itself, and in this sense it highlights the generic decadence of the many earlier Jamesian characters. The delay is allegorized in such a fashion that the inarticulated substance is identified as the 'beast' so that the story itself literally becomes a 'fable' of decadence.

It is characteristic of the Jamesian narrative that a static situation be substituted for action. To rehearse the story, John Marcher and May Bartram meet at a party at an English estate ten years after a previous encounter on the Sorrento bay (when she was 20 and he was 25), remembering only that unfortunately no incident had occurred between them. May remembers that he had told her and only her a secret: that he had felt from his earliest years the sense of being kept for something rare and strange, prodigious and awesome, that sooner or later *something* was to happen to him, something which would annihilate him. The reader knows that Marcher obviously means love, and that he was then anticipating it. Marcher admits, however, that ten years later this wonder had not happened and begs May to watch and wait with him for what he views as the crouching beast in the jungle.

They continue to associate with each other, seeing each other constantly in London, until her impending death (she suddenly develops a fatal blood disease), at which time she admits that she has seen the beast, whereas he has not. In failing to admit his love for her, he had not experienced it. She warns him that it is never too late, but he fails to grasp her beckoning or innuendoes and only regrets that what he had expected had never come to him. How he would have preferred a notorious life to an uneventful one! What he never had then disappears into her death, as May dies. Years later, he suddenly realizes before her grave that *she* was the missed experience that he had failed to grasp. The beast of life had indeed sprung and passed him by, for passion had never touched him.

In this story, two characters conduct a vigil of life in the process of which life is annulled – transformed into death, symbolized in the passing of May Bartram. She represents the potential life spirit which, unseized and unexploited, wanes in futility. As for Marcher, he is the typical Jamesian archetype of the non-participant in life. Like the more developed character, Lambert Strether of *The Ambassadors*, he is marked by an apprehensive attitude toward life, an overwhelming fear to embrace it and engage in an affair with it. Marcher is left mourning the passing of an experience not realized – avoided in the past, and postponed into the future. The story is tantalizing yet disturbing because it conveys an absence so prodigiously. Life is represented existentially as something luscious and pulsating which fails to emerge concretely because of a reluctance to give it recognition. Postponement here eventually reaches total avoidance.

If Dostoevsky painted an idiot gasping for vitality, James

portrays a Decadent who bypasses it. James identifies the most intrinsic aspect of the nature of the Decadent as he probes his characters' ineffectual relationship with life. He divests the Decadent type further than Dostoevsky's religious and cultural archetype or paradigm of decline, to create an actual persona from a salient, pervasive symptom which persists in all Decadent narrative. The negative relationship with life, most blatant in Jamesian characters, seems to be a heightening and moderniza- tion of a Hamlet-like pose of inaction, here expressed in terms of tactics of postponement: anticipation, regret, detour, delay and blockage. Life itself is aborted in the process. The characters are paradoxically engaged in an itinerary which leads nowhere, as highlighted, for example, in the ironic French meaning ('walk') of Marcher's name.

Ironically, in their negative relation to life, such characters gain ascendance as a 'type'. In their rejection of the essential, they become momentous in their triviality. They also, uncannily, approach the characteristic attitude of the Aesthetes, who prefer the imaginary to the real, although their social context is entirely different. What James is especially scrutinizing is a disintegration of intentionality, which he proceeds to express in both form and character.

The gap identified *within* the Dostoevsky character is here viewed more specifically *between* the Jamesian ones, as one of the effects of postponement is ineffective communication. In the early novel, *The American*, this is seen in cultural terms where the two different cultures are incompatible and the resolution of the plot in marriage is not fulfilled between the American and the French- woman. The international theme presents the most obvious barriers of misunderstanding. The lack of communication be- tween Christopher Newman and the old-world Bellegardes emphasizes the distance between the two worlds, which is due not to their physical separation but rather to their moral incompati- bility. The schism rather than the union of the two cultures is brought about by the abiding class distinctions. Here is the so-called decadent European class seen to be stalling and postponing. It is hesitant to accept the active American who thinks that he can acquire culture by his decisive enterprise.

In this novel, James is experimenting with a situation in which Christopher Newman, as the representative of the new world with its raw strength, is trying to captivate the mellowed European world in its presumed decline. But Newman's entry into this society seems to be irrevocably blocked. The 36-year-old self-made millionaire and Civil War veteran, takes a pleasure trip to France to finally enjoy life and purchase a wife as a prize for his hard years of work. He is soon struck by the daughter, Claire de Cintré, of an aristocratic but impoverished French family, the Bellegardes. He readily asks for her hand in marriage. But his intentions are checked, as the family hesitates to give him its consent because it considers him lower-class and foreign.

Paradoxically, where financial prosperity could serve as a blood transfusion to the declining aristocracy, represented by the Bellegarde family, it is not accepted and an ambiguity prevails as to the future prospects of that hierarchy. The moral barriers such as pride, hypocrisy and prejudice are like the physical walls which enclose the Bellegardes's old, obsolete manor making it inaccessible to the new man whose blank past makes him strikingly fresh and open. Newman admits at various points that he fails to understand them. Their social snobbery and aristocratic pride, as vestiges of the past, preclude revisionism and revival.

What prolongs the drama is the long-drawn-out decision-making on the part of the Bellegarde family monolith, and their inability to face the decision once they weakly make it. The dialogues resemble static poses with marked intransigence on both sides. It is true that under duress the Bellegardes assent at one point, lured in spite of themselves by Newman's money to cure their desperate financial status. But that forced decision is subsequently withdrawn, and barriers, both psychological and physical, are once again erected to exclude such a possibility. The situation remains one of impasse. The Bellegardes are unwilling to accept the vigour of the 'new' represented by the Newman character, because they are unable to face the reality of their decline and they do not want to sell themselves short. Consequently, Newman's attempts are in vain. His inability to penetrate the old guard shows him as an inadequate and premature substitute for an established class ascendancy.

In the case of the French, the waning is given the aesthetically defined 'decadent' conventions of disease, decay, flower, which suggest the French rhetorical symbolism of demise. The jaded figure of Valentin represents all the symptoms of a decadent stereotype of a waning aristocracy. His weakness of character and purpose, his intransigent pride and esoteric code of honour are

impediments to transformation, as he is unable to adopt Newman's commercial alternative. His self-infatuation in his love for
his sister removes him from all prospects of marriage and
progeniture. Ultimately, his obsolete value of honour literally
leads to his death as it prompts the emblematic duel which
challenges that nobility and effaces the character representing it.

Valentin's death is matched by Claire de Cintré's seclusion in
the Carmelite cloister. Unable to assent to Newman's prospects,
she withdraws from life entirely. The lily-like woman remains
pure in her inner sanctum as she withdraws from communication
and her growth is stunted by the family's prejudices derived from
an esoteric class structure. An obvious aura of decay, as
symbolized in the dark and impenetrable edifice of the entire
Bellegarde manor, isolates the European culture. The novel
creates a climate of cultural decadence, engulfing the American in
it.

The elements of postponement and lack of communication
apparent in the novel contribute to the Jamesian ambiguity as it is
applied to the ending of the narrative. The American returns to
his homeland, and his future, though not designated as a failure in
any respect, is uncertain. The novel produces an atmosphere of
frustration, especially so because this mood is in noticeable
contrast to what one would expect to surround the good-natured
and active man. The fact that he has failed in attempts at
marriage is a foreboding sign, given the energy, goodwill and
vitality which mark his disposition. The 'luck' which was part of
the Horatio Alger formula for success has been overshadowed by a
barrier to exchange and, as many have observed, this is a comedy
with an *altered* ending.

It is clear that even in this early fiction James was communicating the problematics of Decadence through the structure of a
predicament or impasse. It is true that the simplistic, unselfcon-
scious Newman has none of the procrastinating features of James's
later characters, but it is also noticeable that unknowingly he is
subject to procrastinating tactics which frustrate his ambitions of
success. In constructing the later book *The Ambassadors*, James
proceeds to isolate the theme of a matured man in a quandary of
postponement and stylistically to elaborate the mechanics of
delay.

By the time James wrote *The Ambassadors*, producing a more
complex form of the American character, the figure of postpone-

ment had not only marked and debilitated his hero but had also viscerally permeated his prose. From the position of an observer of decadence in *The American*, he seems to have become engulfed by his subject, and appears to have lost the critical distance from it which he originally had. (This can be accounted for by his habitation abroad and his increased exposure to the European climate.) The dichotomy he had demonstrated between the European who postpones and the American who wants to take action is no longer the case. In the later book, it is the American who suffers from postponement which prevents him from fulfilling a moral mission and makes of him a failure. The focus has shifted from cultural misunderstanding to a psychological blockage. Of course this does not have the implications of a religious mission such as the Idiot's; none the less it exemplifies a commensurate loss of intentionality.

The novel incorporates this factor of postponement which shapes its structure and style in a significant way as well as its principal character's mentality. The novel itself becomes one big postponement, as paradoxically nothing transpires. It seems blatantly to defy plot, that structure of the novel which James was later consciously to consider a nefarious conceit when in retrospect he wrote the Preface to the New York edition of *The Portrait of a Lady*.[1] It successfully gives the belaboured impression of filling up time, in a digressive manner, as it exudes, throughout, a physical sense of long lapses of waiting. Percy Lubbock, in identifying the novelty of James's point-of-view technique in 1921, noted that the novel lacked movement but he did not recognize that this is due to the factor of postponement: '*The Ambassadors* is without doubt a book that deals with an entirely nondramatic subject – it is the picture of an état d'âme.'[2]

The plot itself is postponed in *The Ambassadors*, appropriately so, since action is forestalled by the principal character. Lambert Strether, the 55-year-old widower, is specifically sent on a mission from Massachusetts to France to rescue the son of his widowed and prosperous fiancée from a French woman who is seducing him away from his family and country. It is hinted that if Strether fails in this task, he is nowhere as far as his projected marriage and a propitious future are concerned. In Paris, Strether meets this son, called Chad Newsome, and is attracted instead of repelled by his condition. He demonstrably postpones the confrontation with Chad and leaves the situation in a state of impasse, rationalizing and unconsciously convincing himself that the 'situation' does not warrant interference on his part because it does not exist. He demonstrates a 'detached zeal' and 'curious indifference' in an equivocal attitude toward his errand, thereby abating its urgency. When Strether finally sees Chad and the French mistress, Madame de Vionnet, together on a boat in the countryside, he realizes that he has avoided his duty. When he finally confronts Chad, the occasion has been missed for retrieving the young man, and Strether departs for America: mission failed.

The gait which describes the 'ambassador' Lambert Strether is one of wary strides, hesitant pauses; his are postures of prolonged uncertainty, fidgety gestures of delay. This is highlighted especially in the opening pages of the novel where, upon his arrival in Europe, he hesitates and delays his meeting with his old friend Waymarsh, for fear of being overtaken by the European 'note' off guard, a note totally inharmonious with his customary puritanical tone of deliberateness. He wastes time, so that the exposure will be gradual and the commencement of proceedings be deferred. The style of these opening lines approaches a near satire of the principle of postponement:

> The same secret principle, however, that had prompted Strether not absolutely to desire Waymarsh's presence at the dock, that had led him thus to postpone for a few hours his enjoyment of it, now operated to make him feel that he could still wait without disappointment. (3)

That figure of postponement underlies the many instances of failure which reflect a state of Decadence in *The Ambassadors*. It acts as a contagious germ surreptitiously contaminating the structure of the novel as it characterizes its principal character's movements both from the vantage point of the past (his life in Woollett) and in his 'present' encounters (in Paris).

In *The Ambassadors*, the character Lambert Strether has denied life by 'the failure to enjoy' (16). He persistently diverts his attention from the immediate, turning life into one big digression. Incapable of indulging in the moment, he perversely admits to the enjoyment of the 'duration of delay' (5). 'I'm always considering something else; something else I mean than the thing of the moment' (19). His decidedly absolute 'moral consciousness' limits his activities and is an impediment to a spontaneous and active participation in life. He belatedly mourns the passing of his youth. Hence, in the well-known statement to the youth, Little Bilham, 'Live all you can; it's a mistake not to' (217), he regrets, as did James himself, that he had acted as an outsider and observer rather than as a receptor of experience.

Like Marcher's situation in 'The Beast in the Jungle', Strether's is an irresolute attitude toward life, resulting from his tendency to evade and escape it. A lethargic nostalgia colours his recognition of its passing. He had allowed life to pass him by with a blank, unresponsive attitude toward it. In some respects, this blankness resembles the Idiot's passivity. James depicts this disposition in the following mundane analogy: 'And it's as if the train had fairly waited at the station for me without my having had the gumption to know it was there. Now I hear its faint receding whistle miles and miles down the line' (217). It is a reverberating image which can be repeatedly associated with the Decadent persona.

In the case of *The Ambassadors*, the missed experience is of course crystallized in the Chad–Vionnet attachment as it symbolizes the greater 'affair' of life. Strether's delay ultimately occurs on the level of consciousness as he stalls in acknowledging the truth of the relationship before him. The crucial scene in which he views Chad and Mrs Newsome in intimate company in the boat, vividly stylized as it is, is the closest he gets to a lived experience, in terms of a vicarious substitute of vision for immersion.

Chad becomes representative of the fawn-like object of corruption to which the hero is exposed and against which he takes a weak stand. Referred to as a 'pagan', he joins the company of the Dionysian personalities of Decadent fiction. Like Dostoevsky's Nastasya and Zola's Nana, he is a product of the 'corrupt' metropolis. Here the Babylon is Paris, and for Strether it proves incapable of being 'reformed'. Strether does not seem able to cope with the young Chad, and treats him as do all Decadent heroes in the presence of their modern adversary, as a new 'breed'. His obligation to reform the degenerate youth is not fulfilled, and Strether's inadequacy is stressed in his ineffectual dealings with the Dionysian figure who appears actively engaged in the affair of life. Chad's brazen expenditure is distinguished from Strether's parsimonious disposition. Chad's indulgence in life is contrasted with Strether's withdrawal from it. James goes so far as to note that Chad had no delays.

Strether's cerebral approach to experience conditions his delayed responses, and it is that psychological itinerary that determines the marked character of forestalment in James's prose. James deliberately fails to bring the moment to a crisis in his narrative, and the frequent lapses in time which occur before the 'reckoning' (or encounters with the 'corrupt adversary') attenuate the impact of experience. In the final instance of reckoning between Chad and Strether, another delay is prompted which is described as having the bitter-sweet flavour of reconcilement to death: it serves to annul the relationship between them. Strether muses:

> It amused him to say to himself that he might for all the world have been going to die – die resignedly; the scene was filled for him with so deep a death-bed hush, so melancholy a charm. That meant the postponement of everything else – which made so for the quiet lapse of life; and the postponement in especial of the reckoning to come unless indeed the reckoning to come were to be one and the same with extinction. (293)

Furthermore, Strether's failure to accept the *ficelle* offered to him by Maria Gostrey, a character who represents for James the 'residium' of the plot (as he indicates in his proposal for the novel with the significant date of 1 September 1900),[3] symbolizes the lasting reluctance to tie the strings together of the turgid narrative and the indeterminateness of the final assessment. To have Strether fall into the arms of the devoted Gostrey at the end would acknowledge a realism and conclusiveness which this symbolic prose shuns.

The poetics of delay leads inevitably to another ambiguous ending where again a possible 'marriage' is avoided and a 'ripe separation' is achieved in rarefied prose. Of James's novels, *The Ambassadors* seems to be the most technical in its expression of postponement. The subject itself, the deferred mission, is at the service of form. In *The Ambassadors*, the prolonged delay, the persistent tendency of anticipation, regret and postponement in Strether's character foreshadow from the start the improbability of any concluding action.

In the case of his provocative social novel, *The Portrait of a Lady*, James had earlier expressed in perplexing terms the substitution of delay for resolution as Isabel Archer finally succumbs to a 'failed marriage' after a strained deliberation. This novel is deliberately marked by a 'want of action in its earlier part', as James himself admits in his notebook entry.[4] To what extent James envisaged the imposing character, Isabel, as a procrastinator and agent of postponement is also made clear in his notebook, where he says that the novel's last word, 'wait', is a 'characteristic characterization of Isabel'.[5]

The imperious Isabel shortchanges herself in a social, cultural and psychological context. Isabel does not succeed in fulfilling her intention to assume a new emancipated sexual role. In spite of herself, she remains trapped in the image of a reticent Victorian lady. Of all the suitors from which to choose, she selects the most insipid Philistine specimen among them in the person of Gilbert Osmond, and falls prey to illusion. What makes her failure all the more disturbing are her hesitations and precautions at the beginning not to be duped into a conventional marriage. An aspect of the Decadent element in Isabel's character is her failure to accept the real, as it is tangibly offered to her, and her tendency to grope toward the unknown. Although socially acceptable suitors are offered to her, she selects an unknown scoundrel to reshape with her illusions. Most perversely, Isabel takes a detour to avoid a full commitment to love.

In the beginning of the novel, Isabel Archer, the young American woman who goes to Europe from Albany to visit her cousins the Touchetts at their estate in England, gives signals of a propitious destiny. James assigns the following adjectives to her: beautiful, accomplished, clever, amiable. It is obvious that she is in search of a husband as well as identity. She is very attractive to a number of eligible suitors, including an authentic lord, a wealthy 'commercial' American and even her charming cousin, Ralph. She is determined at the same time to live up to her ideal of independence which she is proud to possess. Presumably, James's problematic character has been exposed to liberal attitudes of the times, like those contained in J. S. Mill's *Subjection of Women* of 1869.

She delays, however, in making decisions, surprising all by her rejection of the aristocratic Lord Warburton because, in her mind, that would be too facile an alternative and restrict her with a social constraint. In the meantime, upon the death of her uncle Touchett, she acquires financial independence by inheriting half of his fortune. This should give her an even greater liberty in her choice of a mate. At this point, Isabel manifests her habit of postponement by the imaginative leap with which she selects the suitor who does not meet the expected requirement. The 23-year-old girl perversely consents to marry the 40-year-old 'good-for-nothing' dilettante Gilbert Osmond, an expatriot American in residence in Italy, for what he lacks: 'no career, no name, no position, no fortune, no past, no future, no anything' (281). It is as if she evades the here-at-hand to surmise the unreal, and in so doing is victimized by her imaginative obstinacy. She only later learns that he is an opportunist after her money and innocence, and when she loses a child in the marriage, she comes to regret the union but is too proud to annul it.

Ironically, her financial security enables her to exercise freedom to delimit herself within the bonds of a constraining marriage and perversely to stunt rather than to nourish the development of her selfhood. She has tended to 'see' rather than to 'feel' and in enacting the social conventions of a worthless marriage remains on the outside of life, having postponed a truly emotional commitment to a man. Isabel seems to be the major female joining the Jamesian gallery of failed specimens such as the Marchers and the Strethers. In these cases, an emotional germination has been sacrificed to an intellectual and aesthetic preoccupation. As the experiential has been minimized, the buds of life have been blighted for these characters. They all remain distinctly removed from life experience, given as they are to excessive reflection which prevents or distorts action. Traces of the complex Isabel will be recognized in the perplexity of Sue Bridehead in Hardy's *Jude the Obscure*.

The novel can be interpreted within the paradoxical context of James's epitaph 'the real thing', which he used as the title of one of his short stories in 1892. An aesthetic proclivity was illustrated there, by which the artist foresook the real for the intended, the actual for the imaginary. The story contains James's famous lines regarding this aesthetic perversity: 'an innate preference for the represented subject over the real one: the defect of the real one was so apt to be a lack of representation. I like things that appeared; then one was sure' (317). Like some of his contemporaries, James was rejecting the Naturalist and Realist tendencies of his time, as in the attack he had made on Sir Walter Besant in 'The Art of Fiction' in 1884. In this respect, James resembles Zola in spite of his distaste for him. James is obviously unaware of the fact that

Zola's Naturalism does not preclude leaps of the imagination so often discernible in his work.

Like Dostoevsky, in his examination of a prototype, James creates an aesthetic expression of the defective. For ultimately, the 'lady' fails to be viable because of that character's avoidance of the real. Here the narrative renders a damaged specimen, as in the striking case of James's *Golden Bowl*, the more sophisticated work which focuses on an imperfect relationship objectively conveyed by a cracked bowl and corrupt Italian prince. A subtle clue to James's stylistic orientation is found in the parable of the decadent artist in 'The Real Thing'. For the artist-illustrator of that story damages his artistic talents by using 'perfect' specimens of the aristocracy for his models. In that story, it is to be recalled that when the artist uses plebeian specimens, from which his imagination can leap, he postpones the real before him, to create the ideal in his art. As the artist suddenly resorts to a perfect lady and gentleman as models for the representation of aristocratic figures, his art deteriorates because that imagination is marred, no longer effectively engaged in surmising the perfection. As efforts toward perfection are annulled, the artist merely illustrates and represents the ideal mimetically in realistic fashion. What especially marks this story is the process whereby this decline is traced. In the case of *The Portrait of a Lady*, the disparity between the real and the ideal, which is maintained, successfully fosters the Decadent style.

While Isabel Archer is no artist, it is interesting that her attitude toward life is an aesthetic one: the constrictions she experiences in her marriage to Osmond are expressed in terms of suffocation and decay wrapped in an aesthetic fold: 'When she saw this rigid system close about her, draped though it was in pictured tapestries, that sense of darkness and suffocation of which I have spoken took possession of her; she seemed shut up with an odour of mould and decay' (199). Such words as 'mould' and 'decay' seem incongruous with the vivid life potential that Isabel exhibited at the beginning of the novel, but they are words which designate her fallen position once she takes some action. A breakdown of her propitious prospects has occurred. She becomes trapped by her solipsistic position, erecting a barrier to life. By shying away from the reality of Osmond to an illusion created by her own imagination, she is performing another act of postponement.

In a curious way, Isabel partakes of the same failing as the Idiot, as she refuses to express that self of hers in material form. This is witnessed in the following lines, where she contests Madame Merle's worldly materialism:

> 'I don't agree with you. I think just the other way. I don't know whether I succeed in expressing myself, but I know that nothing else expresses me. Nothing that belongs to me is any measure of me; everything's on the contrary a limit, a barrier, and a perfectly arbitrary one. Certainly the clothes which, as you say, I choose to wear, don't express me; and heaven forbid they should!' (288)

Isabel refuses to extend herself beyond the limits of her ego, and falls in the Nietzschean category of the 'Despisers of the Body' (see *Thus Spoke Zarathustra*). She betrays the pillar of selfhood associated with the body. In a manner reminiscent of the description of the Idiot, she is described by James as having 'no talent for expression' and therefore falls into ineffective communication. She also fails, as does the Idiot, by refusing society, particularly demonstrated by her reluctance to marry the socially acceptable Lord Warburton. Her obstinate individualism removes her from productive integration.

Though married, Isabel retains the identity of a diffident virgin with intransigent scruples, as she remains enslaved by her self-portrait and cloistered by her egotism. Some might even consider her cold. She admittedly remains rigidly circumscribed in her identity to suit Osmond's cult of appearance. Her initial originality becomes engulfed in the conventional.

When Isabel finally realizes her failure, her lost gamble, her world is dramatically darkened. Her shock of recognition occurs within the setting of the Roman ruins, and is identified with absence and a vanished world of which vestiges only remain. As to be seen in the case of Hardy's Jude, decay itself surrounds the character here, heightening the sense of personal failure by an environmental analogy, thereby uniting the personal with the collective: Jude before the Oxford ruins, so Isabel in the ruins of Rome.

Perversely, the closest embodiment of her unrealized self is that of her dying cousin, Ralph Touchett, who is appropriately of kin, and whom she ultimately associates with the ghost of the

Gardencourt mansion. It is through him that she could have had true freedom and she missed that opportunity. All too appropriately, the character of Ralph is marked by disease, and this state of perpetually impending death is a variation of the theme of postponement. When Isabel ultimately associates him with the figure of the ghost which she seeks unconsciously in her futile quest for selfhood, he is on the verge of becoming engulfed into the missed identity which typifies so many of James's characters. The figure of the ghost, often employed in James's fiction as representative of the alter ego, has already become her foil. Ralph is unattainable not only because he is her cousin, but because he eventually dies. The union necessary to complete the self is aborted.

Fittingly, Isabel's final posture is one of waiting, as she remains 'prostrate' before the dying Ralph, anticipating his death. The final chapter is replete with the word 'wait', and equivalent for the postponement rampant in James's other prose. In this light, the whole novel seems to have spanned Isabel's waiting for the vision of the ghost of Gardencourt which Ralph had promised she was to see:

> He had told her, the first evening she ever spent at Gardencourt, that if she should live to suffer enough she might some day see the ghost with which the old house was duly provided. . . . She had no inclination to sleep; she was waiting, and such waiting was wakeful. (418)

An elegaic tone, regretful and vigilant, colours the ending of *The Portrait of a Lady*, as it does so much of James's prose. This eschatological climate characterizes the ambiguous ending, true to James's aesthetic conviction (stated in a notebook entry) that 'the whole of anything is never told.'[6] Isabel encounters the pallid face of Ralph, her cousin, and like other Jamesian characters, begins to regret what had not passed between them. (The typicality of such a position was to become overtly stated in 'The Beast in the Jungle', as has been seen.) Isabel decorously attends his death, postponed and expected as it is, as if the novel had only dragged out an inevitable occurrence.

Throughout the narrative, then, it is the death of the ailing Ralph Touchett which has been postponed. The character of Ralph becomes an embodiment of the figure of postponement and an effective trope. As the novel ends on the much awaited incident, the sought-after ghost or symbol of romance emerges to disrupt the normative flow of prose and avoid the finality of a definitive ending. Psychologically, the experience of death seems to awaken Isabel's sensitivity to a more visceral relation to life and the possibility of discarding her previous cerebral actions as convention. Her true affection for Ralph, the potential of passion for the rich American industrialist Goodwood, become real factors which had hitherto been neglected. A symbol has emerged as a signalling factor, the possibility of a new relationship has been expressed. The sociological viability of the 'lady' identity has been overshadowed by a failed feminine paragon.

The portrait is thus completed with a blotch of ambiguity, as the characters Isabel and Goodwood remain in limbo. Having recognized that she has been duped, Isabel is ambivalent despite her dogged scruples. It is true that she returns to Rome after the death of her beloved cousin but that return is marked by hesitancy: 'She lived from day to day, postponing, closing her eyes, trying not to think. She knew she must decide, but she decided nothing; her coming itself had not been a decision' (421). The presence of Goodwood in the end intimates a possible, though nebulous, passageway toward retrieval. It is in fact Goodwood who sees things as they are and, in bestowing a kiss upon Isabel, he makes a tangible claim for her. Henrietta Stakepole's final words to Goodwood suddenly become the ringing ones of the novel: 'just you *wait*' (437), she tells him. Though James knew he could be much criticized for leaving the novel up in the air, he insisted that his procedure was paradigmatic.[7] The indeterminate ending is reminiscent especially of *The American* and James's unwillingness to acknowledge and thereby enact satisfying human relationships. The fact that the last word of the novel, 'wait', is uttered by a *ficelle* has structural implications: the resolution of the plot is once again intentionally postponed.

Perversely, then, James's major heroes and heroines fall short because they defer in 'bringing the moment to a crisis', to borrow the expression of the ultimate twentieth-century persona of postponement, T. S. Eliot's J. Alfred Prufrock. Like Prufrock, they wallow in indecisiveness and delayed action as they dodge the significant:

> And indeed there will be time . . .
> Time for you and time for me,
> And time yet for a hundred indecisions,
> And for a hundred visions and revisions,
> Before the taking of a toast and tea.[8]

Interestingly, too, the ghost figure becomes a form of conceit of James's shorter prose, specifically of the *fin-de-siècle* period, of the unattained, the regretted, the contour of the thing postponed, the phantom presence of the thing absent.

In the story 'The Altar of the Dead' of 1895, James crystallizes postponement into absence and exalts it as he constructs an artistic edifice for it. The story describes the situation of a character, George Stransom, who is typically removed from the actual as he communicates with the dead spirits, designated interestingly as 'postponed pensioners' (5). In particular, he communicates with the love he never consummated, a certain would-be bride Mary Antrim, who had died of a malignant fever before her wedding day. She becomes a ghost for George, and for him her absence is more real than the reality of her actual existence: 'for the girl who was to have been his bride there had been no bridal embrace' (3). Figuratively, existence is described as the 'house of which the mistress was eternally absent'. The absence of that character is dramatically felt, as a postponement of presence making life vacant. Ultimately, the persona George embraces the most Decadent attitude in viewing life as a postponement of his own death: a digression.

The Jamesian cast hence is a company of failures, trapped in failed marriages, figurative and actual, and inarticulations and misappropriations. It has been seen how postponement not only appears on this level of character but within the narrative structure as well. There are narrative situations which nullify themselves and a persistent language of delay. The prose, with its characteristic ambiguity, is the spatial equivalent of that postponement of ending.

For ultimately, the dismal fate of a character like Daisy Miller is a fault of representation: in presenting herself in a society by a behavioural code which can be misinterpreted. Symptomatically, James's characters are unable to clarify, emotionally or intellectually, and in detecting this as a default in expression, James himself is quite clear. It is here that his ambiguity wanes, for that ambiguity describes his characters' situation, not his; James stands all too lucid and towering over it. As the poetics of postponement evolve in the Jamesian narrative from *The American* to *The Ambassadors*, James gradually goes from a critical distance to an engulfment by the object of his criticism; but in the final analysis he prevents himself from becoming totally infected by this process of Decadence by becoming self-critical and by the fact that he finds action in writing.

In James's later work, the structures of postponement become relegated to strategies of language, and social textures become less significant – in, for example, the highly intricate *Golden Bowl*. The failure in relationships he discerns seems to result precisely from the outright avoidance of the significant: the detour to the trivial, which is reflected in the terse language replacing action. The characters are marked by their refusal to clarify, as they use language to conceal rather than reveal meaning. Ultimately, Decadence as manifested in James's work was to become a question of semantics. Discourse paradoxically sustained repeated postponement of the admission of inarticulated truth.

4 Emile Zola and the Hyperbole of Consumption

In his panoramic view of French society in the wake of the Franco-Prussian war, Emile Zola created a clear definition of decadence by associating it with indulgence and the loss of control. However, his depiction of material excess was to be stylistic not thematic, the tone moral not moralistic, as he evinced the mechanism of that decadence. In 1880 Zola had firmly proclaimed a manifesto of Naturalism in his treatise on the 'experimental novel', adapting the findings of Claude Bernard and the Positivists to his conception of the novel. There he had stated in principle that the rigours of scientific truth were to be brought to the novel form. But at the time of the publication of *Germinal* in 1885, he had to admit that his art had in fact surpassed Naturalist observation, for his method had actually necessitated an 'agrandissement de la verité' (an exaggeration of the truth). In a letter to Henry Céard, he states: 'I have the hypertrophy of the true detail, the leap into the stars from the springboard of exact observation. Truth rises on wings up to the symbol.'[1] In tune with his times, Zola used a physiological metaphor here to illustrate the enlargement process of his artistic expression to which social reality was subject in his fiction. Described in terms of the abnormality of 'hypertrophy' this symbolization became his telling testimony of the decadence within.

Through the hyperbole, Zola actually isolated and catalyzed the elements of his conception of Western decadence which highlighted the contagious quality of an excess whose overall pervasiveness cut through class structures and social distinctions, a germ so to speak which assaulted and affected all the levels of society. The consumption-ailment which debilitates the whole can be identified as the major symptom of Decadence: 'In society as in the human body, there exists a solidarity which unites the different parts, tying together the different organs, such that if one organ decays, all the others are affected and a very complex sickness is announced.'[2] In concentrating on physical analogies such as the capitalist mine in *Germinal*, the body in *Nana* or the alembic of alcohol in *L'Assommoir*, to name a few, Zola featured agents of hyperbolic consumption.

The French word 'appétit' serves Zola in a number of ways, both in actual physical connotation and in a figurative one. Ever characteristic is the 'débordement des appétits' (overflow of appetites) in the Zola canon. 'Manger' is the all-purpose word used to render consumption concrete. Zola uses its nineteenth-century Darwinian connotation of struggle for survival to high-light the deterministic quality such consumption assumes. The notion of the 'gros' or flabbiness is frequently used to connote the underlying weakness of will and moral lassitude. What results is a deterioration of character (both stylistically and psychologically) as a general spread of fatigue moves across class distinctions. This aspect of excess is particularly striking in *Germinal*, where the moral inadequacies and debility of a ruling capital class are duplicated in the labour sector in a simultaneous process. This procedure creates a mutual impression of mechanistic void through the omnipresent visual quality of the central image and the structural determinism of the seasonal sequences.

The portrayal of the mine, 'Le Voreux', voracious as the name itself, is from the beginning of the novel conceived as a dark mouth consuming the energy and stamina of the workers it engulfs. The mine is impersonated as a crouching beast with apocalyptic powers and consumptive activity: 'And Le Voreux, at the bottom of its pit, crouched as an evil beast, churned more, exhaled with a longer and heavier breath, the air disturbed by the painful digestion of human flesh.'[3] Throughout the novel it is depicted as 'repu' (stuffed) yet eating with a gluttonous appetite that is never satiated. As characters are destroyed within its midst, the mine itself represents inordinate consumption and in bestial fashion it externalizes the eating away or attrition within the social fabric. A dark womb-like receptacle of human specimens, it churns and gorges the human element and harbours agents of its own destruction as it is ultimately envisaged bursting into an apocalyptic deluge. The mine is the pivot around which destruction occurs; in the process of consumption it is itself consumed.

Zola identifies the destructive forces of the mine as a weakness from within. For if the mine abuses the human services and reduces the workers to beastlike insects, it is also unable to sustain itself. This is evidenced in the initial fact that the mining company has to contract some of its work: 'The worker might be dying of hunger, but the company also was eating into its millions' (1335). For the old mine gives signs of structural weakness. It is as if the seams of Le Voreux, which fall apart, transcribe possible points of vulnerability and waning within the capital class. In terms of imagery, Zola incorporates the decadent stereotype of the Barbarian assault on Byzantium in his description of the mining disaster to suggest the paradoxical situation of capital at its apparent height. This expression of decadence, focused as it is on the condition of the mine, identifies the 'germinal' imagery with the blatantly destructive scene in the vision of the dreamy Etienne Lantier:

And in this awaiting of a new invasion of barbarians regenerating the decayed nations of the old world, reborn was his faith in a coming revolution, the true one, that of the workers, the flames of which would burn up the *fin-de-siècle* with the red glow of the rising sun now drenching the sky in blood. (1589)

The rhetoric of *fin-de-siècle* with its purple tones describes a state of transition. The notion of the old order waning into the advent of the new, although still anticipated, is communicated as a dominant mood. This atmospheric effect of a waning age is particularly shared by Zola's contemporary, Thomas Hardy, whose emphasis is less political than moral. In setting a moralistic past against a 'moraline-free' future (to use Nietzsche's terminology) Hardy proceeds, as shall be seen, to explore the impact of such conflict, not upon society, but upon the individual. In the case of both Zola and Hardy, an analogy is established between an old world and an old edifice. And whether it be the decrepit mine or the crumbling walls of the Oxford edifice, the structures are dramatically conveyed as decaying.

Eschatological paradigms colour Zola's works, as the collapse of the dark mine, Le Voreux, exceeds the proportions of an individual mining catastrophe, representing symbolically a challenge to the system. It is significant and disturbing that action is in

the hands of the anarchist Souvarine, whose act of total destruction actually effects the mining collapse and moves the novel to its
cataclysmic ending. The attempted and belaboured designs of the
characters Etienne Lantier and Rasseneur, the socialist
revolutionaries in the variant modes of evolutionist and progressive, are instantaneously surpassed by the nihilistic attitude of
Souvarine which surfaces at the end, and gains ascendancy as the
name suggests. He is envisaged physically attacking the mine in
its entrails and actually creating the deluge. In some ways his
response resembles the devastating one of the ominous Father
Time in Hardy's *Jude the Obscure*, as will be seen. Like Souvarine,
Father Time's dispassionate 'mechanical creep' ('he followed his
directions literally without an inquiring gaze at anything'[4])
effectuates action in an otherwise stalemate situation of ratiocinative stalling, and thereby precipitates the narrative to the
catastrophic forecast of impending doom. In the case of Zola, the
image of the mine, collapsing and expiring as a giant monster
gorged with human flesh, is hyperbolized in the proportions of an
apocalypse, with paradigms of beast and deluge prevailing.

Throughout the novel and leading to the ultimate catastrophe,
Zola's technical patterns of duplication and mirroring highlight
the decadent process harboured in the mine. If the bourgeois is
signified by the brioche cooking in the oven, the working-class
household is seen craving and consuming a lower form of bread.
The kitchen is another piece of reality which Zola seizes upon in
symbolic fashion as a locus of consumption. To use George
Poulet's approach to morphological metaphors, the process of
consumption here receives another spatial objectification. This
milieu and ambience create an exaggerated effect.

The 'immensity' of the Grégoire kitchen and its gourmand
table, identifying the bourgeois stereotype, is cast hyperbolically
as the centre of activity:

> The kitchen was vast [*immense*] and by its scrupulous cleanli-
> ness and the arsenal of saucepans, pots and utensils which filled
> it, you could tell that it was the most important room in the
> house. It had a goodly smell of food. Racks and cupboards were
> overflowing [*débordaient*] with provisions. (1195)

The plump and spoiled child Cécile is its symbolic product. In
contrast, the Maheus are cramped in their household, engaged in

eating their crumbs of bread and begging for more to fill their 'ventre vide': 'Catherine was pondering in front of the open cupboard. All there was left was a bit of bread, plenty of cream cheese, but only the merest shave of butter' (1149). Jeanlin's avid hunger is representative of their offspring. It is typical of Zola to express class struggle in the politically charged terms of the 'gras' (fat) versus the 'mince' (thin), as indicated in the notes to the appropriately entitled novel *Le Ventre de Paris*. But what is stressed in the later novel, *Germinal*, is the compounding of the consumption process in the society as a whole beyond the issue of class conflict, as a deterministic factor of general decay. The ironic counterparts of the eating process converge most strikingly in the well constructed chapter of the Hennebeau luncheon party for the Grégoires at the time of the strike. The intent is to bring together Cécile Grégoire and Hennebeau's nephew, Paul Négrel, joining the 'corpulent' sector. There the series of courses of an enormous meal is given utmost attention, proceeding with the precision of clockwork. When news of the threatened strike is flashed, the idle and stout Madame Hennebeau responds in irresponsible fashion: 'Oh, so they are on strike. Oh, well, what difference does that make to us? We aren't going to stop eating, right?' (1304). Indeed, a whole sardonic chapter passes in the uninterrupted consumption of a menu of truffles to coffee while workers continue their obsessive struggle for bread.

In myriad forms, consumption appears as a focus for excess. The violent and bestial death and emasculation of the company's grocer, Maigrat, symbolic of his function as the source of food, is yet another instance. As the workers take vengeance on one who had cruelly refused to offer them sustenance in times of dire need, they draw attention to the central factor. From their consumptive drive, uncontrollable behaviour erupts. The consumption and the destructive element are joined, and the results are as devastating in this individual instance as the collapse of the mine. In the case of the Maigrat affair, the theme of promiscuity and consumption are linked in the fact that La Mouquette, the symbol of inordinate sexuality, is the agent of the grocer's horrific emasculation.

Such violent forces surge throughout the novel, most readily conveying the destructive and consumptive element at work. Promiscuity is seen to be equally present and contagious in the cornfield as in the bourgeois household. For example, Etienne is disturbed by the frenzy of the lovemaking in adjacent quarters: 'It

wasn't that it prevented him from sleeping, but they pushed so
hard that in the end they were damaging the wall' (1241).

The rampant sexuality throughout *Germinal* is likened to a form
of consumption, exhaling a heated atmosphere like that of
ovens and mines. La Mouquette, the sexual symbol, who has
countless affairs and even manages to win Etienne over at one
point, is a form of monstrous power. The overt sensualism is an
obsessive factor invading the bourgeois sector as well, exemplified
in the case of the Hennebeau household. The little interlude
describing Madame Hennebeau's adultery and Monsieur
Hennebeau's sense of personal failure remains a haunting scene.
It is through Hennebeau that Zola expresses the analogy of
consumption: in discovering clues to his wife's affair with his
nephew Paul Négrel, Hennebeau ponders in disdain that her
illicit sexuality has become a form of incessant consumption:

> By now it had become simply a depraved amusement, men had
> become a habit for her, a recreation, like dessert after a meal.
> He blamed everything on her, almost exculpating the boy
> whom she ate into, in this arousal of appetite, as one might bite
> the first green fruit picked up on the road. Whom would she
> devour [*mangerait*] next – just how low would she sink, when
> there were no more obliging nephews? (1432)

Ironically, however, the upright and incompetent Hennebeau is
envious of the carefree sexual activity of the masses before him.

The deterministic aspect of these various forms of excessive
consumption is metonymized in the phrase 'la nécessité du
ventre', as the belly becomes the one constant amidst the
variables. Its expression as the struggle for survival is highlighted
by the symbol of the rabbit, Pologne, which is discovered *eaten* in
the fields, and its analogy with the human Jeanlin whose struggle
for existence leads him to an unscrupulous killing of a sentry. It is
also the inner necessity which returns the workers to work without
any progress as they forego the tactics of the strike. And when
Etienne contemplates future worker rebellion, he expresses it in
the Darwinian terms of future consumption as an unending
process of survival and competition:

> Wasn't Darwin then right; wouldn't the world be a battle, the
> strong ones eating the weak ones, for the beauty and perpetua-

tion of the species? . . . If one class had to be devoured, wouldn't it be the people who would devour [*mangerait*] the bourgeoisie, weary of pleasure? (1589)

The activity inherent in the multiple connotations of the word 'manger' converges into the continuous consumption hyperbolized and causing the 'dégringolade' (decadence, downfall) and the 'avachissement' (flabbiness, lack of energy) – powerful words which translate the crumbling and the waning.

This rampant hyperbole has the effect of paling the stylistic delineation of character. This phenomenon has perhaps been overlooked by the classic Marxist objection to Zola's work. Lukács, for example, sees no historical determinism in the individual characters whom he regards as psychologically *private* types with private histories unintegrated in any social process. Interestingly, he objects to the fact that they are not individual or concrete enough as authentic social types. He does not find social institutions dissolved into personal relationships and functioning as bearers of class interests as he does in Balzac. In his *Studies in European Realism*, Lukács contrasts Zola with his preferred Balzac: 'The basic rule which Balzac follows is to focus attention on the principal factors of the social process in their historical development and to show them in the specific form in which they manifest themselves in different individuals.'[5] He asserts that in Balzac, social forces never appear as superhuman symbols or fantastic monsters as they do in Zola. Nor do social institutions appear 'romanticized' in what he calls the subjective abstraction of Zola's mechanical (rather than dialectical) analogy between the human body and human society.

Lukács eventually attributes Zola's alleged failure as a social realist to the fact that 'the ideology of his own class was too deeply ingrained in his thinking, his principles and his creative method, although the conscious sharpness of his criticism of society was never dulled'.[6] This he contrasts with the case of Balzac who, presumably a Royalist, was subject to the determination of his own historical epoch which made him, in his exposure of the inherent contradictions of nascent capitalism, uninhibited by the artificial effects of class rubric. More recent critics such as Jean Borie[7] have also noted Zola's attraction to Utopian socialism – which is not in concordance with their belief that Zola's work reflected the actual process of socialist development.

Critics like Lukács do interpret Zola's work along with that of other Naturalists as evidence of a 'decadent' stage in capitalist literature, but they single out the pejorative connotation of the word 'decadent', as it departs from what they regard as the authentic vision and technique of socialist realism. They do not perceive that it is the captured ambience of decadence in the case of *Germinal*, for example, which determines the plot and diminishes the integrity of the individual character types above and beyond their identification with a class structure. In fact, an Etienne Lantier can be identified with an Idiot or a Jude in common symptoms of weakness, regardless of social milieu.

Specifically, the process of duplication and mirroring in *Germinal* has demonstrated a collective texture of human ineffectuality emerging. The characters remain pallid, sharing common traits of listlessness, self-destructiveness; they are on the verge of waning into oblivion. Their individual identities surface in initial form, soon to fall back into the common pool, as in the case of Etienne who remains always bland and faceless, a pale paradigm of failure.

If the mining environment turns the oldest member of the Maheu family, Bonnemort, into an automaton consumed and conditioned by its operation, it reduces the youngest member, Jeanlin, to the dehumanized condition of an animal, surviving on instinct and impulse in a ruthless race for food and sex. Bonnemort, as suggested by his name, is a living figure of death, whose ancient appearance belies his 58 years. Jeanlin is likened throughout to a roving rabbit force with primitive drives, which eats and multiplies. He assumes, too, the features of a fawn-like creature, reminiscent of a Dionysian archetype which is a familiar motif in Decadent narrative; Etienne contemplates him:

> The young man was silent, his mouth full, troubled. He looked at the child who, with his pointed muzzle, green eyes, long ears, resembles some degenerate with the instinctive intelligence and craftiness of a savage, gradually reverting to man's animal origins. The mine, which had made him what he was, had finished the job by breaking his legs. (1370)

Both Bonnemort and Jeanlin are eventually killed by the consuming mine.

Before the mine, humans become insignificant as they lose their individual identities and form a file of shadows trailing into darkness. The fact that Etienne, as the leader of the strike, is not given a central position stresses the failure of individuality amidst greater collective forces. He remains positioned at spatial and psychological distances from his objectives; his long purviews of the mining scenes emblematically remove him from effective involvement in the workers' cause. His character never burgeons; nor has it impact on his surroundings. A similar 'obscurity' of individual character is crystallized in Hardy's Jude, as will be seen. There, a physical distancing also conveys a gap between aspiration and its fulfilment. Etienne's failure is exemplified in the paradigmatic way in which he recovers his initial position as a peregrinative wandering labourer seeking work at the end of the novel, in futile, unprogressive motion.

Etienne's contradictory position contributes to his metaphysical and literary marginality, and as a character he remains very much the observer, like many of the Decadent personae. The hypocrisy with which he espouses the workers' cause while at the same time aspiring to the position of a leader with eventual bourgeois ambitions is an inconsistency which causes his failure. The conflicting tendencies within him, created by the conflicting social climate without, make him inviable and ineffective.

Like the Idiot archetype before him and the Jude figure after him, his character becomes diluted through a prevailing inadequacy caused by passivity and lack of initiative. In fact, in a position analogous to that of the Idiot, Etienne fails both in a 'mission' (here a political one rather than a religious one) and in a relationship with a woman: Catherine. His inability to communicate verbally is stressed repeatedly as a factor contributing to his social ineffectiveness. His reticent and timid nature makes him lose his beloved Catherine to the more aggressive and possessive Chaval, who steals her from under his eyes. His inherited tendency toward alcoholism which surfaces periodically at crucial moments that require full attention is comparable in its effect to the epileptic bouts of the Idiot. It renders him unable to deal with crisis situations.

Etienne's mental activity is also marked by a theoretical and abstract approach which distances him from the reality before him. He is given to musing and dreams, socialist theories and Utopian hopes, instead of action and implementation. Zola's indirect discourse highlights this. Symbolically, also, Etienne is often pictured pondering books and treatises, in static postures.

Yet to overscrutinize the personal deficiencies of an Etienne Lantier is to attribute psychological depth to a character in a novel which is in the very process of transforming individual character into paradigm, released from previous moral codes. The lean and timid Etienne remains a shadowy figure on the verge of assuming a collective identity. What distinguishes Etienne is that he becomes a failure in the development of a new social archetype rather than the weakening of a previous, recognizable model such as the religious one of the Idiot. The character of Etienne is in draft form even as the social structure into which he has been situated.

In the case of *Nana* (1880), often regarded as an ornamental period piece of the Second Empire's blatant 'corruption', it can be seen how the heroine's white body specifically becomes the target of the hyperbole. Nana enacts the 'nervous exaggeration of the sexual instinct' (Fauchery's article, 1269). Her personality is indeed subservient to her physicality as she becomes the personification of sensual excess. The individual character surpasses its individual significance, as it assumes a mythical dimension, conceptualizing whoredom. Character has lost its concreteness here not because it has become a pale paradigm of failure but because it has become a powerful conglomerate of sensual forces and has attained a mythic role. Zola obtains an overt and uncontrolled sensuality debilitating an entire social corpus. The literal and spectacular way in which Nana is shown infecting and destroying an entire society is the effect of stylistic exaggeration. She becomes a living emblem of appetite and waste as she 'feeds' irresponsibly upon the men in her midst and is never satiated. The consumption analogy with sexuality here receives prime treatment:

> What remained, in the hours when she was not indignant, was an ever open *appetite* of expenditure along with a natural contempt for the man who was paying, and a constant caprice of *consumption* and waste which took pride in the ruin of her lovers. (1349–50)

The word 'manger' is used with reference to her voracious sexual appetite as she becomes a 'devourer of men' (*mangeuse d'hommes*) eating up acres of property, heritages and professions by the mouthful – 'à chaque bouchée, Nana dévorait un arpent. . . . Le triomphe de Nana fut de l'avoir et de lui manger un journal' (1455–6). Zola brings a series of victims to Nana's caprices from various segments of society (journalists, bankers, counts) and hyperbolizes her magnetic power of attraction. Her most symbolic conquest is that of Count Muffat; she becomes therewith a catalyst for the decay of the aristocracy. In the metaphor of the golden fly, she is reported to be the agent of corruption as she spreads the squalor from the people to the aristocracy: 'corrupting and disorganizing Paris between her white thighs' (1268). It is as if Zola is demonstrating as literally as possible his dictum: 'if one organ decays, all the others are affected and a very complex sickness is announced.' From the sordid grounds of Naturalism a leap to symbolization has occurred in the presentation of this alluring and 'supernatural' character that vividly engulfs a whole society. Her destructive force reflects the failings of that society.

It is interesting to note that in some respects, Zola is here not far from his Aesthete contender Huysmans in the creation of monstrous metaphors to express sensuality. The 'Grande Vérole' or Pox is the hyperbole of disease in *A Rebours*. But where Huysmans resorted to mechanical women and lacquered erotic looking flowers suggesting the pox, Zola created a living, natural creature of sexual excess in the person of Nana. Whereas in Huysmans, the association between the pox and the artificial flower expresses the analogy between sensuality and art as possible avenues of escape from reality, in Zola it is this very reality of the social decay that is the target of his stylistic expression of sensuality.

If Nana is mythic rather than individualized, her character is stylized by exaggerated poses. Though written earlier, *Nana* seems to amalgamate the sensual forces and drives which surface sporadically in *Germinal*. The repeated metonymic images of her haunches, neck and the bed are the realistic parts which undergo hyperbolic treatment and create a cult of sexuality. The Byzantine bed outrageously replaces the altar. The self-infatuation of the narcissistic prototype, a kind of Salomé or *femme fatale*, is captured in physical terms:

Nana was absorbed in her self-enrapture. She was bending her neck and looking attentively in the mirror at the little brown mark which she had on top of her right haunch. . . . Slowly she opened out her arms, suggesting the torso of a corpulent Venus. She stretched out her figure, examined herself before and behind, stopping to look at the contour of her bosom and at the fullness of her thighs. (1270)

Fittingly, she terminates this anatomical self-examination of neck, hips, torso and thighs with motions comparable to a belly dance (*danse du ventre*): the consumption reference returns. The presentation of Nana in her boudoir receives an arabesque and ornamental treatment, comparable to the elaborate sequences and detailed descriptions that were designated as true decadent style by the Aesthetic stylists of the term. But the Dionysian ecstasy which the character Nana achieves in her self-contemplation is devoid of creative energy because of her compulsive self-consciousness. Instead it leads to destruction, evidenced by the facts of the narrative. One of her liaisons results in miscarriage. And the final image of Nana is that of a rotting corpse which, like the images of Nastasya in *The Idiot* and later Kurtz in *Heart of Darkness*, portends the decadence of the social structure.

The apocalyptic paradigm also becomes associated with this work, as Nana is likened hyperbolically to the biblical beast of the Revelations in the mind of the infatuated Count Muffat:

He thought of his old horror of Womankind, of the monster of the Scriptures, of the lubricious and the bestial. Nana was all covered with fine hair, the soft russet made her body velvety; whilst the Beast was apparent in her equine flanks and buttocks, in the fleshy bulges and depressions which endowed her sexuality with the provocative mystery of their shadows. She was indeed the Golden Beast, an unconscious force, whose odour alone corrupted the world. (1271)

The language used to describe Nana's bestial allure is provocative in its sensuality and visual effect. The outrageous scene in which the Count prances on all fours before Nana is reminiscent of the image of the Harlot of Babylon and her beast in the Apocalypse, identifying in the waning of Second Empire France a paradigm of moral corruption. As in the instance of *The Idiot*, the biblical reference is invoked directly and elaborated upon in the novel's expression of social decadence.

In the case of two other social and political novels of the Rougon-Macquart, *L'Assommoir* (1877) and *L'Argent* (1891), the consumption metaphor permeates the language and remains the unifying expression of the decadence which Zola observes. If in *Nana*, the signifier is the body, in *L'Assommoir*, it is the drinking dive. The alembic of alcohol in *L'Assommoir* receives hyperbolic description and the proliferation of the substance it contains literally translates the Decadent effects. As Nana's sexuality pervades the streets of Paris and destroys the aristocracy, so the liquid of the alembic floods the streets and debilitates the working-class population, contributing to the specific deterioration of a certain worker family:

> The alembic, noiselessly, without a flame, without a disturbance in the reflections of its dull copper, was sweating out alcohol, like a slow and persistent spring which would eventually pour out into the room, spread to the outer boulevards, and inundate the immense cavity of Paris. (411–12)

Here, Zola is literally enacting the 'hypertrophie du détail vrai', as he focuses on the alembic and its alchemy into symbol. A mysterious quality is ascribed to this container in its transformation from a real observed object into a signifier by the exaggerated spread of its potent fluid. The excessive consumption of alcohol suggested by the obsessive intrusion of this signifier implies the universal weakening of will-power and the aggravation of an already inherent lassitude in the total population not exempting the working class. This is illustrated in particular in two members of the working class, Coupeau and, finally, his wife, Gervaise, the laundress. The Naturalist observation has been transformed into symbolic representation as the alcohol passes through the catalytic container to harbour Decadent effects: 'And the shadow cast by the machine on to the back wall created abominations, figures with tales, monsters opening up their jaws to devour the world' (704). The symbolic 'leap' has been enacted, and the consumptive power of the drinking dive is expressed through its association with monsters opening their enormous jaws to devour (*avaler*) and with a cauldron 'round as a belly' (*ventre*) (706).

As the reality of the drinking bar L'Assommoir (which

harbours the alembic) acquires a symbolic dimension, the word 'assommer' expands semantically into its various connotations. In particular, the signification of weariness is attached to it. The word in its meaning as 'bludgeon' denotes a weapon used to beat and overwhelm. In the context of the novel, it alludes particularly to conjugal quarrels often caused by excessive drinking – when men beat their women. The meanings 'drinking bar – bludgeon – overwhelm' carried by the highly allusive word 'assommoir' describe the situation. Gervaise's attempts to arrest her husband's degeneration are defeated by an overwhelming sense of fatigue within her, which develops from her many ordeals. The young woman, mistreated and abandoned by her former lover and father of her children, Lantier, is coerced into marriage with a 'vaut rien' of a zinc worker who drains her of her energies, with anguish, while consuming himself in alcoholism. The forces are greater than the pathetic figure can endure, and she appears tired and beleaguered, burdened well beyond her 22 years. As in the case of *Germinal*, an immense fatigue weakens and consumes the human specimen. Zola here generalizes this condition to describe the corrupt society's effect through the analogy of a bludgeon actually used: 'Her dream was to live in an honest society because being in a bad society was like being bashed on the head; it cracked your skull open and reduced a woman to less than nothing' (417).

Another symbolic aggrandizement is that of the 'machine à vapeur', the steam engine located in the giant laundry shed. In an arresting paragraph describing the laundry scene, Zola conveys the oppressive environment through the cumulative power of detail. The prose follows the same expansive procedure used to describe the mine in *Germinal*, the body in *Nana* and the alembic in *L'Assommoir* and markedly echoes these other engrossing descriptions, starting with the static, copulative 'c'était . . .':

It was an immense laundry shed, with a flat roof. . . . A heavy moisture rained down, charged with the smell of soap, a stale, dank, persistent aroma; at times the stronger odour of bleach prevailed . . . the steam engine, on the right hand side, white with a fine dew of condensation, puffed and snorted incessantly. (386–7)

Here not only are the visual qualities magnified, but those of odour and sound are intensified. The combination of odours of bleach and soap with a milky fog of hot stream creates a suffocating atmosphere. In a further spectacular hyperbole, the whiteness of Gervaise's laundry extends like a sheet of blankness across the urban scene mirroring the way the blackness of the mine pervades *Germinal*'s rural scene with darkness. Like the mine in *Germinal*, the mechanistic objects in *L'Assommoir*, the 'machine à souler' (the alcohol machine) (704) and the 'machine à vapeur' (the steam machine), are envisaged as agents generating excess and consuming the human element in the process.

L'Assommoir demonstrates the breakdown of resistance, as it were, with respect to a disease. Zola scrutinizes the slow but steady process of decline through the figure of Gervaise. Placed in an environment of already deteriorated specimens, in the company of Lantier and Coupeau, she slowly loses her control as she imbibes the spirit of lassitude around her. Her ambitions of constructing a laundry boutique to support her dependent household are soon defeated; as the debts of her miserable store mount, the more heedless and lax she becomes. In a striking section of the novel, Zola gives physical signs of her moral deterioration. As her lassitude and irresponsibility increase, she becomes more corpulent and sordid: 'she too was getting too fat' (*elle aussi devenait trop grasse*) (647). As in the case of Madame Hennebeau of *Germinal*, though in a different social context, her external flabbiness expresses an inner looseness: 'she let herself go' (*elle s'y abandonnait*), 'she lost her integrity' (*elle perdait de sa probité*) (644), 'they were consuming her' (*ils l'usaient*) (648). The manner by which she becomes oblivious to the increasing sordidness and putridness of smell (*puanteur*) around her is another sign of her deterioration. Zola turns her into a grotesque specimen, drastically expressing her state as one resembling unconsciousness: 'a torpor of lassitude' (*engourdissement de fainéantise*). An accumulation of his favourite 'decadent' synonyms exaggerates this particular case of decline with the alliterative *d* sound prevailing: 'dégringolade' (fall), 'débandade' (slackening), 'débâcle' (collapse), 'démolissement' (demolishing) – all of which seem to be summarized in the powerful word 'assommer'. At the end of the novel, Zola depicts Gervaise in a scene at L'Assommoir where, after fervently seeking the irresponsible Coupeau, she loses her own will-power. Forgetting her myriad responsibilities, she succumbs to the vitriol of the drinking dive, the ultimate catalyst of her decline.

The hyperbole in this novel highlights the process of demoralization through the contagious factors of lassitude and loss of control. This consumption-ailment aggravated by the effect of the alcohol is viewed as spreading from Coupeau to Gervaise and eventually to Nana, who was bred in this environment and used to spy on the drunken scenes. As already seen, it is then transmitted by Nana to the Count Muffat in the subsequent novel. One weakness breeds another, as Zola conveyed in an organic analogy in his theoretical treatise, *Le Roman expérimental*. Here it is not a case of duplication as it is in *Germinal*, but of multiplication of effects, and the fluid alcohol is the metaphor for such intemperate proliferation.

Finally, in the novel *L'Argent*, the hyperbole is applied to money: wasteful expenditure is viewed in terms of promiscuous speculation and that excessive spending is part of the hyperbole of destructive consumption. If in *L'Assommoir* Zola isolates the working-class scene in his scrutiny of consumption, when he comes to the writing of his lesser-known novel, *L'Argent*, fourteen years later, he takes on the financial sector. Furthermore, *L'Argent* recasts the dialectics of *Germinal* along an ideological plane. Here the focus is no longer on the contending position of labour versus capital, but rather on the process of capital consumption and the resulting deterioration of the productive capacity of society. In presenting the dialects of capitalist behaviour, Zola places money in the pivotal position of love: 'Why make money bear the burden of the corruptions and crimes of which it is the cause? Is love less tainted, that love which creates life?' (398). But the multiple analogies of love and money in this novel express inordinate speculation in the terms of prostitution. Zola is concerned with the distinction between the accumulation of capital and its wasteful expenditure – accumulation being a constructive process whereas excessive spending is part of the hyperbole of destructive consumption.

At the heights of his commercial success, Saccard and his wife Caroline lyrically muse upon their money, envisaging it as a 'pluie d'or', showering all of Paris with dazzle and golden lustre. The hyperboles are applied to gold, depicted as reigning as a king or god over society. Its abuse in overt speculation precipitates financial failures that are likened to an apocalyptic destruction. Zola evokes the spirit of the end of the world. Eschatological imagery is associated with this excess: 'But this time, behind the reddish vapour of the horizon, in the distant crises of the city, there was a great hollow cracking, the rumbling, approaching end of the world' (361). Zola traces the destruction of a whole financial empire, and the association of empire with the 'banque universelle' (fittingly named) and the portrait of Saccard as its emperor exaggerate the dimensions of its sudden collapse. The vivid description of Paris as a colossal place harbouring a night of debauchery creates a Roman aura of overt decadence: 'like a colossal palace in which debauchery was active until dawn' (253). As for Saccard, the archetypal speculator, he represents once again a mechanism, a chemistry characteristic of a society propelled by appetite, in which speculation is viewed as a necessary 'fattening' (*l'engrais nécessaire*) (382). Rather than simply determine him as a product of his society, Zola conveys him as its extension. This principal character, as in the case of *Germinal*'s Etienne Lantier, is a type rather than a personality. Much less is known of him than of Stendhal's Julien Sorel, for example, whose psychology is explicitly conveyed by his author. As has been seen, Zola subordinates psychology and character to plot and issues in his determination to observe and indicate an eschatological, gruelling spirit of an age, the diagnosis of which seems to be hyperbolic consumption.

Nana's wasteful expenditure is mirrored in that of Saccard's, her male counterpart. Both register factors created by the chronic instability of the time; both serve as personifications of the social body mechanism. Their mythlike identities serve as measurements of the typical condition. What becomes disturbing is that the singularity of their individual cases is anulled as it becomes applicable to the general condition; and the exaggeration which their specific cases imply becomes descriptive of the rule rather than the exception.

Flesh and money blatantly invade Zola's landscapes; and eating along with copulating become the principal activities, as they climactically burst into hyperbolic dimensions consistently throughout the novels. In *Nana*, the body becomes the imperial throne, praised and revered as it proceeds in its increasing conquest and debilitates several sectors of the ruling class, most notably the nobility. In *Germinal*, the mine, physically lodging the private capital, grows to outrageous dimensions of mouth, belly (*ventre*) and beast, consuming in this instance labour and contributing to its 'avachissement' or fatigue. In *L'Assommoir*, the destructive meaning of the word 'assommer' receives attention as the wine and alcohol are agents debilitating that working class, already weakened in lethargy. This is paralleled in *L'Argent*, where the wine analogy is replaced by the gold one: showers of gold (*pluie d'or*) and liquid money (*l'argent qui coule*) flood the city of Paris, having in their intensity the semblance of a superhuman force.

What ties these various facets of social decadence together is the element of excess, expressed in the stylistic method of magnification. Zola's narrative is infected with the germ of hyperbole just as James's narrative is contaminated by the figure of postponement. In each case, the germ assaults the materiality of the text and becomes ingrained in its structure. It affects the contours of narrative and becomes the telling indicator of the Decadence – whether it be the failure of participation, as in James, or the height of indulgence, as in Zola. In his magnification of selected individual objects – the wine, the body, the alembic, the money – Zola creates explosions of gargantuan proportions, encoding the abnormality of Decadence.

Myriad examples of this process of hyperbole can be located in the gamut of Zola's novels, as an identifying trait of continuous consumption and collective drain. It becomes clear that this observation is not limited to the particular problems of Second Empire France, because the symptom of moral flabbiness detected across the various social sectors is a common concern of modern industrial societies, and is evident as well in the other novelists here considered. Zola's spectacular and grandiose visions of decay, with the histrionics of the crumbling and the ruin, seem to pave the way for the colossal catastrophes envisaged by a Conrad. The French author and his contemporaries used a set of metaphoric devices to convey their sense of decadence. In the particular case of Zola, the loss of moral containment was relentlessly expressed in the hyperbole of consumption.

5 Thomas Hardy and the Chronic Crisis Syndrome

As a writer closely attached to his native countryside of Dorset, Hardy was harshly exposed to the dramatic change and slow attrition in his rural environment. From that local vantage point, he proceeded to identify a graver dislocation as he voiced a cosmic concern for the fate of Western man in conflict between the old and the new at the advent of the modern world. Looming in his poetic imagination of the Wessex universe are the haunting images of the heath and the Oxford spires which are the focus for the traumas of change. Hardy absorbs into these two arresting images a debilitating *malaise* caused on the one hand by the physical realities of the invading industrialism on the contemporary scene and on the other by a spiritual ebbing of theology and metaphysics. These disturbing signs of mutated meanings create a moral discomfiture in Hardy which is serially reflected in his novels in what one might call a chronic crisis syndrome. This is the index of his englobing Decadence.

Study has shown that the ideological conflicts occurring on the European continent had their equivalent in the intellectual debates proceeding from the Victorian world; Hardy perceived a loss of mooring in their wake. As the sensitive writer Virginia Woolf has aptly stated, Hardy was 'doomed to see the faith and flesh of his forefathers turn to thin and spectral transparencies before his eyes'.[1] First in *The Return of the Native* (1878), Hardy observes the defilement of the natural landscape: the physical statically testifying to a cosmic shift in orientation from sympathy to indifference. Then disturbingly in *Jude the Obscure* (1895), his most problematic novel, Hardy detects the Western intellectual tradition in a position of remoteness and distance perplexing rather than serving to edify the belaboured humans in their moral and metaphysical concerns. From the Oxford edifice of Gothic Christian values, a disquietude of uncertainty is disclosed,

73

communicating a burden of awareness and its concomitant condition of stalemate.

The moral turmoil prefixed by such Victorians as Mill and Arnold in their discourses is transfixed by Hardy in 'decadent' situations of aggravated complexity. For Hardy is not as confident as the Victorian intellectual optimists just prior to him in the forces of secular culture to fill the gap created by the loss of faith. In this respect he is close in affinity to Dostoevsky, who despite his immersion in the Positivist intellectual currents of the time eventually rejected the cult of Rationalism as a substitute for a waning spirituality. Because of their basic nurture in Christian purist tradition, of Anglican as well as Eastern orthodoxy, both writers proceeded to focus upon the fate of the pristine in the changing times. Their creation of Decadent types emerged from this standpoint of the Absolute. The 'science' of Hardy's fiction, to borrow his own expression from his well-known article of 1891, isolates in individual telling instances the effects of the challenge of the old order by the new upon those specifically nurtured in the traditional faiths. If Auguste Comte created phases to chart the process of evolutionary meliorism, Hardy was as historical in creating a stage in the evolution of sensitivity which can be viewed as 'decadent', corresponding to the crisis in late Victorian culture. Hardy expressed this *malaise* in narrative structures which present matrices of frustrations. For if, as J. Hillis Miller has stated,[2] the Victorians were experiencing the disappearance of God and losing their Romantic structures, Hardy most vividly detected the traumas of detachment from that harmonious pre-established order.

With similar effects to that of the structure of postponement in James, the recurring situation of crisis in Hardy's prose drains his major characters of their vitality and drive and creates a problematic of action in the novels. For whatever paths these stigmatized spirits take in their compelling moral excursions, they are invariably beset by obstructions along their rural peregrinations. The problematic characters of Hardy's Wessex universe seem to be caught and painfully entangled in webs of perplexity between sets of values in chronic crisis syndromes. Hardy's characters become embodiments of a certain traumatic awareness created upon the arrival at what he discerned as a historical crossroad in human destiny. Because of his consciously grasped dichotomy of matter versus spirit in the universe, Hardy becomes practically allegorical in his characterization, which consists of poetic representation rather than distinct psychological depiction. Characters are typecast, such as Tess, the raped, Father Time, the force of destruction, Sue and Jude, the colossal inconsistencies. The simplicity with which their significance can be identified belies the philosophical material with which they are created to represent various facets of the crisis situation.

Hardy's early work, *The Return of the Native*, provides the 'decadent' landscape from which the crisis syndrome burgeons. Before T. S. Eliot's wasteland correlative, Hardy envisaged the heath as an apt terrain for the drama of decadence which his novels enact. As Hardy well knew from the countryside surrounding his native Bockhampton, the heath was atmospheric and evocative in effect. In *The Return of the Native* he identified Egdon Heath as 'the vast tract of unenclosed wild' which joins the beginning and the end of the race – awaiting the 'final overthrow'. Described as a waste capable of exhaling pitch darkness and bearing traces of Celtic origin, Hardy regards it as an obsolete superseded landscape. Also figuring in the medieval *Domesday Book*, it is a locale appropriate to a final reckoning. Specifically, Hardy associates Egdon with a chronic sense of crisis foreshadowing a terminal one. He thereby gives this physical territory a metaphysically portentous character: 'Every night its Titanic form seemed to await something; but it had waited thus, unmoved, during so many centuries, through the crises of so many things, that it could only be imagined to await one last crisis – the final overthrow.'[3] This 'awaiting' is similar to the sense of forestallment ever present in James's narrative. The portentous element associated with the deferment of ending in both cases is made more obvious in the Hardy narrative with the Domesday reference. Furthermore, whereas the postponement of ending is filled by digression in the Jamesian case, it is filled by crisis in the Hardy one. In this respect, the heath provides a spatial dimension for the syndromes. Hardy's reference to a 'final crisis' with respect to the heath endows this physical environment with a historical authenticity which ultimately relates it to his contemporary humanistic crisis. Both in time and space, Egdon is poetically envisaged as a transitional territory.

The preternatural quality ascribed to the heath heightens the realistic terrain with symbolic intensity. Hardy projects into its observable aged condition the fate of Western man in his eschatological position. Appropriately, the first person to alight across it is an old man who bears 'an appreciable quantity of human countenance'. The heath provokes the power of association: it is itself compared to a blank face and allegorized in 'antique brown dress' (6). This natural landscape has the same affective power as Conrad's forest scene in *Heart of Darkness*, which also provokes a host of associations. Here Hardy joins the primal with the final, sets the primitive against the civilized, and meditates upon the collective aging of the human race. He refers to the growing acceptance of the notion of quandary, germane to the human condition, but aggravated in the humanistic crisis of modern times: 'What the Greeks only suspected we know well; what their Aeschylus imagined our nursery children feel' (197). The corrosive fatigue accumulating over the centuries is eventually carried by the child, as later evidenced in the symbolic character of Father Time in *Jude the Obscure*, who reacts to the crisis situation in a nihilistic way.

Awesome and alluring in character, the heath thus represents the raw canvas upon which Hardy ironically sketches the figures who participate in the drama of decline. It is upon this existential soil that Hardy imposes spectacles of falls and declines as his Adams and Eves move as sceptres across the primal heaths. The blank surfaces bear the imprint of 'protracted and halting dubiousness'. This Jamesian sense of warded delay hovers over the area as if to postpone the sociological extinction of the particular form of terrain. Far from the pathetic fallacy of a Romantic landscape, this environment represents a natural fallacy: mutable yet static, colourful yet uniform, imbued with a natural magic by which Hardy characterized his predominant anomalies, adding psychic and symbolic intensity to naturalistic description. It is an index of atmosphere, a physical, inimical setting which encourages the weakening of moral stamina and the attrition of his characters.

This turgid terrain appropriately harbours the marked ambiguity of the Hardy characters in the 'transitional hour': their position is identified with a kind of limbo state. A dark Dantesque colouring marks the rapid change before him, afflicting his native countryside and its inhabitants:

> Then the whole black phenomenon beneath represented Limbo as viewed from the brink by the sublime Florentine in his vision,

and the muttered articulations of the wind as complaints and petitions from the 'souls of mighty worth' suspended therein. (17)

This shadowy atmosphere ironically highlights the moral uncertainties marked upon the visages of the local people as a predominant protean tone. The precarious position of the reddleman is a sign of a local population threatened with extinction. The modern turmoil of unrest corroborates the social changes of the scene, as reflected in the romances of Thomasin, Wildeve, Eustacia Vye, Clym Yeobright, which are demonstrably unsuccessful. These characters become perversely entangled in the heath's atmosphere of dense obscurity which is ready to obliterate the human element.

The physical scenery is imposing, metaphysically diminishing the personages to unaccommodated states. In a simply poetic way, it is reminiscent of the divestiture of Lear and Edgar on the heath. In Hardyesque terms, it serves to dramatize the ontological erosion. It turns Thomasin, for example, into a 'pale-blue spot in a vast field of neutral brown' (187). It dehumanizes Clym to an insect-like state, as for instance in the scene where he labours as a furze-cutter and appears as a parasite of the furze and turf in the eyes of his mother, Mrs Yeobright. It distances characters like Eustacia, who recede into it and are effaced by it. Ultimately, its nearby pools engulf innocent maidens like Eustacia herself. In overshadowing humans in its midst, it produces a series of 'atmospheric' characters. The novel's landscape seems in an existential manner to begin the process of modern diminution of character, moving away from psychological realism toward what the critic Ortega y Gasset[4] has viewed as being the aesthetics of philosophical dehumanization.

Hardy uses the heath as a physical correlative of a moral condition. Encumbered with the vegetation of fern, furze, lichens and moss, it is viewed realistically as an uncongenial place which exhausts humans, entangling their feet and wearying their steps across it. As such, this physical, natural presence contributes to the moral weakening which generally besets the characters. It functions in a manner analogous to the dark mine in *Germinal* in its overt naturalistic presence and similar reductive effects, levelling the human element to the natural. In the case of Hardy, the natural is represented as the elemental with which the individual is at odds, and his heath is a microcosm of a universal and impersonal reality challenging individual identities with incertitude.

Closely associated with the heath are the two unsuccessful lovers, Eustacia Vye and Clym Yeobright, whose amorous uncertainties reflect the tonal ambiguities of the terrain and become paradigmatic of the restless times. Like many of Hardy's women, Eustacia Vye retains a mythic identity; presented as a modern Proserpine in 'winter dress', she seems fatalistically inseparable from her environment. The lethal atmosphere of the heath is duplicated in her dark and deathlike aura and, as in the case of the heath, Hardy elaborates on the morbid evocativeness of her presence. Her bodily contour seems to evoke a mood as her being is more affective than psychological. In this respect, she resembles the phantom-like tainted women of Aesthetic painting and Symbolist poetry, more mythic and idealized than real. Ophelia-like in her drowning, she evokes the morbidity of a Hamlet syndrome, an undercurrent which will be most relevant to the ratiocination which contributes to the Decadence of *Jude the Obscure*. As an Olympian nocturnal spirit, yearning for romantic fulfilment, verging on the carnal and withdrawing into isolation, she is victim to her own inconsistencies and presages the more realistically portrayed figure of Sue Bridehead in the later novel.

The languor and torpor evoked in the manifestation of Eustacia's heavy eyelids seem to be descriptive of a condition more sociological than personal, associated with a Decadent fatigue or *mal* of the *fin-de-siècle*. Her dark, luxurious hair is associated with Western decline: 'it closed over her forehead like nightfall extinguishing the western glow' (75). Her character seems archetypal as a culmination of age-old beauty and romantic provocativeness. She incarnates a general weariness of life, which accounts for her vagrant attitude, and results in her disdain for living: 'No, it is my general way of looking. I think it arises from feeling sometimes an agonizing pity for myself that I ever was born' (232). She also harbours the notion of the kind of imperilled beauty which the critic Mario Praz has identified as a pose of morbid sensitivity characteristic of the decadent period and crystallized in what he has observed as the prevailing prototype of the *femme fatale*.[5] Eustacia's attitude indeed is jaded as it expresses the theme of sterile love and the fallacy of Romantic expectation:

'Yet I know that we shall not love like this always. Nothing can ensure the continuance of love. It will evaporate like a spirit, and so I feel full of fears' (232).

In his turn, Clym Yeobright bears the modern grimace of pensive turmoil. His blank face, reflecting the substratum of the heath, registers the perplexities of the age. Like many of Hardy's figures, he is wrought with the anxiety of analysis, as he returns in this particular instance to his native territory having been exposed to the ethical changes of his times in his excursion to the capital of culture: Paris. Advanced in his thinking he returns a complex character, attempting vainly to conciliate his new exposures with his innate, instinctive proclivity for his provincial environment. His weak attempts to establish a school in Egdon for the local populace show how unsuccessful such conciliation proves. Hardy turns this individual identity into a representative, historical one, as he envisages Clym as a sociological product of the epoch, marked by the fatigued countenance of modern man:

> The view of life as a thing to be put up with, replacing the zest for existence which was so intense in early civilizations, must ultimately enter so thoroughly into the constitution of the advanced races that its facial expression will become accepted as a new artistic departure. (197)

His face is made to bear the burden of a humanistic crisis which Hardy proceeds to describe as the quandary of 'the modern type' (197) facing an indifferent universe and metaphysical loss. In this historical perspective, Hardy is locating what will be regarded as an archetypal expression of decadence, which he designates as 'modern'. It is a visage which will become fully identified with the Jude expression of the later novel. It surpasses the specifically religious dilemma which characterizes the Idiot's expression.

It is interesting that Hardy's expression of Decadence is here measured by an aesthetic gauge; for he views it in terms of the loss of physical beauty caused by the anxiety registered in the pensive visages. On the universal substratum represented by the heath, aesthetic values associated with Hellenism – that is, classical criteria – are displaced by this new modern countenance, borne by a race which has aged. Hardy thereby vividly chronicles a decisive shift in the aesthetics and corresponding sensibility of Western man. Clym Yeobright seems to be one of the characters upon whom the imprint of that shift is registered. Of the writers considered in this study, Hardy thus seems to be most consciously the historian of moral change, as he constantly refers to previous ethical and aesthetic systems – Hellenic, Judaic and Christian – which in his view are in the process of becoming anachronistic.

The psychological and spiritual effects of this crisis in values became apparent in the weakened condition of the major characters. There is a general and pervasive sense of weariness which afflicts them at a time when a virile attitude is needed to sustain the change. This affects in particular the condition of romance, as the lovers restlessly shift their affection from one to another, lacking the attentiveness and persistence needed to form lasting bonds. Crisis situations emerge constantly, as in the beginning of the novel when the intended marriage between Thomasin and Wildeve does not occur, or at the end when Eustacia, suffering from 'ennui', impetuously leaves Clym to flee with her previous lover, Wildeve. These disturbed and beleaguered personages, in contrast to the minor, unconscious and unprobing heathfolk, create an awareness on the part of the reader of an emerging decadent sensibility.

Hardy communicates the moral discomfiture of his characters through physical weakening, making of the metaphysical a physical expression, transcribing the moral into physical terms. In its topography the heath represents an earthiness, as nature is no longer a reflection but an absorption of human symptoms. The characters are entangled in an intricate nexus of nerve fibres. In dramatically positing the meeting of naked existences, of phantom beings, of haunting presences with ghostlike limbs, Hardy observes efforts at communication at problematic junctures and precarious crossroads.

Tess of the d'Urbervilles (1891), a work following the conventions of romance rather than innovating any Decadent structure, introduces in a single instance the weblike sense of crisis that moulds Hardy's narrative. A more focused consideration of moral perplexity is witnessed in Tess's situation, which dramatically begins in Alec d'Urberville's act of seduction – the new upstart from the industrial breed imprinting himself upon the natural, rural specimen that is Tess:

> Why was it that upon this beautiful feminine tissue, sensitive as
> gossamer, and practically blank as snow as yet, there would

have been traced such a coarse pattern as it was doomed to receive. . . . An immeasurable social chasm was to divide our heroine's personality thereafter from that previous self of hers. (91)

Hardy seizes upon the sexual act as an apt expression of a critical moment, as Yeats does later in his poem 'Leda and the Swan'. The experience leaves a mark on Tess, not only because she has 'transgressed' and lost her innocence in the conventional moral sense but because, from this, she is beset by a 'cloud of moral hobgoblins' which interfere with subsequent action. The individual instance has social ramifications; Hardy himself had conceived, in a similar manner to Zola, the interrelationship between the social body and the individual one in his statement of 1886: 'one great network or tissue which quivers in every part when one point is shaken, like a spider's web if touched.'[6] Tess's gossamer-like tissue indeed extends to those around her once she is stigmatized by an unrelenting mark of perplexity. She is first unable to revive her failing family by securing a legal alliance with Alec d'Urberville, a possible transfusion of physical and financial force. She is subsequently rejected by the prejudices of the prototype of Victorian secular rationalism, Angel Claire, who represents a stage of ethical evolution of the times. The result is that she becomes an endangered species in a changing world.

Tess's moral scruples are connected with the decline of a once-aristocratic family and the erosion of the family name from its notable Norman namesake d'Urberville to the common Durbeyfield. At one point, Angel Claire remarks to her: 'I cannot help associating your decline as a family with this other fact – of your want of firmness. Decrepit families imply decrepit wills, decrepit conduct' (297). He proceeds to view her as the 'belated seedling of an effete aristocracy' (297). Though these are the words with which Claire rationalizes his disapproval of Tess's behaviour, they do correlate a psychological weakness with a decaying social state. Tess is susceptible to a marked passivity, expressed in terms of neglect, inadvertence and lack of persistence. A detail assumes sociological proportions: 'she was inexpressibly weary' (86). Tess's fatigue, caused by the excessive demands of the agricultural work which is fast turning her into a labourer, is a factor that contributes to her surrender of moral stricture. At the same time, however, a certain element of aristocratic pride, which she maintains despite her fallen social condition, prevents her from securing a place in society through marriage. She all too readily accepts Claire's callous attitude toward her and allows herself to endure one crisis after another without protest or rebellion. Although the context and setting are very different, Tess resembles the Idiot in her failure to fight for her sociological survival. In both instances, a social displacement determines the behavioral patterns.

The keynote for Tess is the perverse, made evident at the very beginning of the novel when Hardy ironically envisages nature as defective. It fails to provide for the apt meeting of desire and necessity, putting along Tess's path the wrong and misfitted match in the person of Alec d'Urberville. Against this inimical and typical Naturalistic backdrop, it is fitting that Tess should herself be trapped while 'going against the grain'. For from the recognition of the natural defect emerges the modern quandary of consciousness. Once violated, Tess enters a post-lapsarian phase in a world which itself has shunned Christian grace. Hardy comes close to identifying Tess with a fallen Eve, engulfed in a fallen world. Her innocence becomes victimized in a sacrificial Christ-like way but the setting of Stonehenge and its pagan connotations at the end of the novel obviates the possibilities of Christian redemption.

In tracing a steady process of decline in terms of the disruption and dislodgement of the Durbeyfield family, the novel takes the form of a saga chanting the waning of an old guard. Upon the death of Tess's father, the family is forced away from its local village. In the background, there loom atmospherically the remains of the old d'Urberville castles and graves of their presumed Norman ancestry: Tess's last days reflect the ending of that line. Alec d'Urberville smugly testifies: 'the old order changeth' (465). One is reminded of the weakened condition of the Jamesian Bellegardes with the pale Valentin, dying into extinction. But Hardy, as a historian of Decadence, isolates the particular crisis of a family as representative of a critical 'moment' in a metaphysical as well as a social way. For in Hardy's scene the shift in social order has impact on the natural condition. And the character Tess serves as a matrix for such change. Her natural religion is being replaced by a new ethical code which divorces the moral from the religious, removing the mystical quality and replacing it with a new rationalist ascendancy. The countercurrents which must be contended with are dramatically expressed by the cold logical deposit of an Angel Claire and the instinctual energy of the ascendant Alec d'Urberville. Tess herself represents the basic natural element, a 'soul at large', in rural dress in the process of being undermined by the new social influences. She is Romantic nature adulterated and defiled – in metaphysical terms, natural beneficence being destroyed by a lurking indifference and malignancy, by the 'insouciance' of an Alec or the callousness of a Claire. In this manner, Tess provides Hardy with a personification of a passing era in his local scene.

When Hardy finally arrives at the conception of Jude, he has reached the thicket of perplexity. The philosophical tone of this novel conveys most poignantly the universal level which Decadence encompasses, surpassing the social and religious contexts of the previous works. If such works as *The Idiot* and *The American* present cases of moral perplexities, *Jude the Obscure* distils the situations to their problematic essence. Whereas the drama of crisis experience relied upon natural landscape for its expression in Hardy's earlier novels, it surges to the territory of the consciousness in *Jude the Obscure*. In this way, Hardy's grammar of Decadence is most forcefully conveyed through an unalleviating sense of perplexity as he intellectually locates his characters within an atmosphere of waning faith, lost principles and uncertainty. The conflict and struggle of the problematical character, Jude, who is caught between two worlds and is engaged in a combat for existence, highlights a critical stage best described in Hardy's own words as a 'chaos of principles' (394). If there is an outward structure to convey the webs of the mind, it is found in the architectural and geographical constrictions of the novel which compound the thwarting effects of the crisis syndrome.

It is significant that Jude is derived from his namesake in the Bible's Book of Jude, which was cast on the occasion of a crisis. Then, heretics threatened to join the Christian Church, and in response to these apostates, the writer Jude had written a tract, appealing to the Christians to dismiss them and maintain their own orthodox faith. Like Hardy in the wake of Oxford compromises, the original Jude appealed to the unadulterated faith and principles of his religion. In this perspective, Jude represents a purist, orthodox figure, attempting to combat adulteration of his spiritual pursuits. Furthermore, the modern Jude's obscurity reflects the anonymity of the ancient apostle, whose identity is nebulous in the Bible. Hardy transcribes that obscurity to the case of his modern Jude, who is orphaned in both social and cosmic terms. Of working-class background, he is a *natural* orphan who lacks familial background (both parents are dead and had been incompatible in their lifetime). He seeks desperately to ally himself with a cultural heritage of the Western world which, ironically for him, is in jeopardy of being devalued. A metaphysical orphan, he suffers the modern trauma of being rendered a 'peripheral ephemeral' in a universe which has been bereft of its diety and of purposeful direction. What renders this situation most painful is Jude's awareness of his condition and his constant sense of crisis which impedes productive action on his part.

In the light of the 'illumined' obscurity and atmosphere of crisis afflicting the pure, Hardy is able to concentrate upon Jude's inconsistencies in an excruciating quagmire of inaction and stalemate. For Jude belies his lower-class identity as he leaves the carefree existence of Marygreen for Christminster. He then wanders from the outskirts of his Oxford working habitat to breathe the air of stultifying Oxford ratiocination which exhumes a heavy atmosphere of reflexive questioning and meditation. Jude not only becomes an archetypal figure, comparable as many have noticed to a modern Hamlet, but is also a pose. 'Sicklied o'er with the pale cast of thought', he is immobilized. He is easily envisaged, slouched in a corner of an Oxford wall with bent elbow, thinking.

The series of tensions on which the novel focuses frustrate Jude's longing for intellectual and ecclesiastical pursuits and prevent fulfilment of his cultural ambitions. In aspiring to two avenues, Oxford scholarship and ecclesiastical dogma, Jude seeks to add structure to his otherwise stray existence. But poignantly, contingencies of reality intervene and thwart progress toward his goals of becoming a classical scholar and a Doctor of Divinity. In a state of constant tension between the real and the ideal, Jude falls passively victim to the realities immediately before him and, as in the case of the Arabella episode at the beginning of the novel, is unable and unequipped to deal successfully with them. In this respect, he is comparable in his maladroitness with the Idiot, and it is interesting that his second love, Sue Bridehead, actually calls him a 'tragic Don Quixote' (246) – the analogy that Dostoevsky himself had made for his Idiot figure, in his designation of a destructive idealism. Jude can also be associated with a Jamesian persona of postponement, because of his basic fear of life and withdrawal from active participation in it, admitting to himself: 'I am fearful of life, spectre-seeing always' (181).

Jude spans the range from Hebraism to reformed Christianity in his desperate and futile attempts to assimilate the culture in demise before him. Emerging from the limits of Oxford in the working-class district of St Silas, he encroaches upon the Oxford structures, only to be faced with barriers to entry because of his class and weak financial position. Upon his first exposure to Oxford, the stonemason Jude focuses upon the symbolic rottenness of the stone:

> Down obscure alleys, apparently never trodden now by the foot of man, and whose very existence seemed to be forgotten, there would jut into the path porticoes, oriels, doorways of enriched and florid middle-age design, their extinct air being accentuated by the rottenness of the stones. It seemed impossible that modern thought could house itself in such decrepit and superseded chambers. (92)

In this atmosphere of a failing culture, Jude becomes an even more isolated being, and perceives himself as a ghost amidst other ghosts. In a Jamesian way, he begins to feel the presence of a superannuated past in the form of 'mournful souls' and 'nervous movements'. His conception of Christminster is an idyllic one, echoing the great paeans to Oxford which are ironically undermined by Hardy's portentous comment:

> He did not at that time see that medievalism was as dead as a fern-leaf in a lump of coal; that other developments were shaping in the world around him, in which Gothic architecture and its associations had no place. The deadly animosity of contemporary logic and vision towards so much of what he held in reverence was not yet revealed to him. (99)

Deluded, and avoiding the reality before him, he imagines himself speaking with the Oxford luminaries when, in fact, he remains totally outside communication with the scholars. At a later point, Jude superimposes the image of his lost love Sue Bridehead (once she is married to Phillotson) upon the Oxford scene which is unattainable, thereby associating one inaccessible phantom with another. By this act of transference, he personalizes the cultural situation in his Shelleyan vision of the ethereal, 'disembodied' Sue, who reflects the spiritual twilight of the times. Jude's inability to possess Sue fully is another facet of his distance from his ideals. For in spite of her liberal protestations, she remains, in her integral presence, an essence of bygone times.

The Oxford backdrop is one of a set of institutional constructs of academic and religious signifiers, which Hardy presents as having lost its medieval vitality and significance. Indeed Marcel Proust has noted an architectural recurrence of certain patterns in Hardy's plots which create the impression of a certain sameness in configuration and mood.[7] This is certainly true of *Jude the Obscure*, where the protaganist encounters one environment after another 'from which life is visibly departing' – and is critically affected by this. As Jude proceeds from Salisbury to Shaftesbury, having demonstrably renounced his religious ambitions by burning his theological books, he meets yet another setting in decay. The medieval town of Shaftesbury, renowned for its churches and shrines, is presented in a state of 'general ruin' and, in the face of such decrepitude, Jude gradually renounces his occupation of cathedral masonry for the more lowly task of stone-cutting in the light of modern priorities. By the end of the novel, he appropriates the environmental weakening into his own spiritual atrophy, as his academic books lie useless beside his dead, dehydrated body.

The recurring crisis at the heart of *Jude the Obscure* is the fierce and perplexing battle between the flesh and the spirit, which Hardy himself overtly mentioned in the preface to the novel. This debilitating conflict is tangibly lodged in the antagonistic position of the two women, Sue and Arabella, and it is the effect of these competing categories which blocks Jude's mental progress. Because of the dichotomy of his own ontological view, Hardy separates Sue and Arabella instead of viewing their natures as two aspects of a single individual. He places Jude in a limbo state between them. Jude's encounter and sporadic relationship with the two women, hence, creates intermittent crisis experiences throughout the novel.

The most striking of these experiences is of course the initial incident when the local farm girl, Arabella, throws a piece of pig flesh in Jude's path: a dramatic and symbolic gesture of carnal intervention. This is comparable in impact with the initial crisis experience of the former romance, *Tess of the d'Urbervilles*. It is seen how Jude shows little resistance to this first sexual encounter and succumbs readily to the crude and proximate forces of reality, which are new and transitory to him. Hardy notes that Arabella's life has nothing in common with his own, except locality; and ironically it is this insignificant coincidence which traps him. The portentousness of this experience is shown in the repercussions: the forced marriage which ensues and the deterrence from the intended track. Jude ponders deterministically the resulting entrapment: 'He was inclined to inquire what he had done, or she lost, for that matter, that he deserved to be caught in a gin which would cripple him, if not her also, for the rest of a lifetime?' (71).

With Arabella, Jude is exposed to what are expressed as crude, unconscious forces of reality which gruel in the underbrush and emanate from the procreative environment of the agricultural scene of Hardy's Wessex countryside. Jude's inactive, reflective position is highlighted in strong contrast to Arabella, who represents all that is non-thinking and primitive, yet ever constant and vital. Motivated by primal forces and urges, she succeeds in leading a complacent life, devoid of the scruples of moral awareness which her lover Jude experiences. It is seen how she ruthlessly engages in the gross activity of the killing of pigs, as the daughter of a pig-breeder, whereas the sensitive Jude, whom she embroils in a relationship, is incapable of killing a bird. Active in the most basic toil of making a living through physical labour, Arabella is robust, resilient and firmly equipped to manage the scheme of survival. She is comparable in her primal forces and sexual drives with Zola's character Chaval or Dostoevsky's Rogozhin. The trick by which she catches Jude and her practical usage of the legal procedures of her society to her advantage in terms of her marital affairs makes her part of the material medium which catalyzes the kind of situations leading to the syndrome of Decadence.

As Hardy's prototype of the 'complete and substantial female animal' (42), Arabella is one of the forces at odds with the ideals of finer, spiritual aspirations. She is representative of a vital force which Hardy's weaker characters are unable to accept and appropriate. Uncomplicated, lacking any perplexity, she is the one to survive the challenges of everyday existence, exemplified in the fact that it is she who utters the last words of the novel, predicting the dismal fate of the ill-equipped Sue Bridehead.

Arabella's emotional shallowness is evidenced in the final scene, when she leaves Jude lying dead in his room and engages in fraternity with the local workmen in a festival in Christminster. It is that insensitivity which proves to be the source of her resilience.

Not only is Arabella debilitating with respect to Jude, but she perpetrates through her offspring with him an ominous and gradually deteriorating state leading to total devastation, which Hardy substantiates in the concrete and unambiguous character of Father Time. As an emblem of 'Age masquerading as Juvenility' (332) this amoral imp comes to foresee the avatar of the human on the way to an apocalyptic time-bomb. It is through Father Time, a character totally obsessed by death, that Hardy personifies his eschatological element. He draws a young character who paradoxically embodies an aged vision of the human condition and through him suggests the nihilistic response to the stalemate. The striking, critical scene in which Father Time kills two children and himself without any trace of moral restraint is due to the objective logic of perpetrating extinction, fostered by indifferent nature, turning the chronic crisis into a terminal one. This character provides for an ultimate extension of the Decadent tendencies he witnesses and serves as a catalyst for the undetermined plot.

Father Time's destiny lacks the pathos of tragedy, because there is here a complete eradication of feeling. Hardy refers to the 'impersonal quality' of this 'mechanical' figure, comparable to the indifferent aspect of the 'movement of the wave, or of the breeze, or the cloud' (334). In the words of the doctor summoned to diagnose the case, Hardy expresses his sociological fears, as he regards this specimen as a new breed of human being likely to emerge in the evolution of the species: 'The doctor says there are such boys springing up among us – boys of a sort unknown in the last generation – the outcome of new views of life. . . . He says it is the beginning of the coming universal wish not to live' (406). This statement presages Hardy's eventual cataclysmic vision which marked his later most pessimistic years wherein he predicted war. Jude's descendant seems to echo the Schopenhauerian death drive which haunted so many of the writers and poets of the 1890s in their artistic expression of the life metaphor. The alternative provided by Father Time is a definitive response to the chronic crisis syndrome which besets the major characters of Hardy's fiction.

For the truly Decadent types in Hardy's universe are not the Arabellas or their offspring who forcefully enact their views with no hint of lethargy, but the 'colossal inconsistency' (210) of Jude Fawley and Sue Bridehead. Hardy presents the two as human beings in vacillation, and their failure in life situations is due to this marked indecisiveness of their natures. In a letter of 20 November 1895 to Edmund Gosse written from Max Gate, Hardy discloses their pathological tensions:

> Of course, the book is all contrasts – or was meant to be in its original conception . . . Sue and her heathen gods set against Jude's reading the Greek Testament; Christminster academical, Christminster in the slums; Jude the saint, Jude the sinner; Sue the Pagan, Sue the saint; marriage, no marriage.[8]

The prevailing crisis is manifest in the way the characters imbibe the ferment of the epoch and its inconclusiveness: the failure to surpass the Christian–pagan dichotomies with a post-Christian synthesis.

This crisis is made concrete in their interpersonal relations. Sue Bridehead, a mirror-image of her cousin and lover Jude, compounds his ambiguities and proceeds to aggravate and intensify his problematic situation. Jude's own idealized vision of Sue heightens the dichotomy he observes between the flesh and the spirit and makes him unable to reconcile these two conflicting factors in his relationship with her. Hence, his inner turmoil and indecision. Both in physique and in intellectual make-up, Sue remains intangible and disembodied for Jude because of the contrast he construes with the seizable, tangible animality of Arabella: 'So ethereal a creature that her spirit could be seen trembling through her limbs, he felt heartily ashamed of his earthiness in spending the hours he had spent in Arabella's company' (224). Nurtured in the readings of the classics and with a marked tendency toward abstraction, the cultivated Sue Bridehead is viewed by Jude as a creature of civilization: an epithet which seems to be a euphemism for Decadence rather than a cultural ideal. As a complex character who indeed harbours many of the competing currents of time, Sue's ideology and religiosity is at a puzzling stage: she is referred to as a 'conundrum'. Ranging as she does from being a blasphemous

disciple of Swinburne to a Christian convert and penitent at the
end, she explicitly incarnates a crisis in values.

As static and perplexing as Jude's pose is the vignette
circumscribing Sue's pagan idolatry in the telling scene where she
fancifully admires her pagan idols of Venus and Apollo, holding
them up before the statue of the crucifix in a gesture of outright
defiance. Associations of the more blatant decadence of the 'finis
Latinorum' are evoked in the mention of her reading Gibbons's
section of Julian the Apostate and Swinburne's 'Hymn to
Proserpine'. Like an apostate herself, Sue extracts the following
ironic lines from that foreboding poem:

> Thou has conquered, O pale Galilean
> The world has grown grey from thy breath! (111)

The poem is in tune with Sue's spiritual crisis since it captures a
moment of transition with a dirge-like aura of waning faiths and
foresaken creeds. Its larger focus as a paean to death itself, with its
reference to Proserpine, reflects Sue's own Decadent nature. An
aura of Antichrist reigns in Sue's shunning of the Gothic which is
before her and her scorn of the medieval which her lover Jude is in
the process of renovating in his masonry of the deteriorating
Oxford edifices. This ultimate discordance created by the restless
shifting of faiths, where Jude is attempting to restore what Sue is
out to demolish, creates an irony in their relationship.

In keeping with this ironic logic, Jude's eventual abandonment
of theology for unfulfilled passion is prompted in particular by
Sue. She would not on first glance be considered an obstacle to his
spiritual progress since she represents to him the heights of
spirituality in her being. For though she boasts of pagan
self-assertion, she acts true to Christian self-denial in spite of
herself. Her effect upon Jude, however, continues the crisis
syndrome initiated by Arabella. This is demonstrated in his
climactic burning of his theological and ethical books shortly after
his Aunt Drusilla's death. Then he fully admits to himself his
desire for Sue and its discordance with his religious dogma and
intention to enter the ministry. He is perversely drawn toward
Sue, who is emblematic of the conflict in values as she herself
harbours an internal warfare between flesh and spirit, between
progressive and reactionary ideals – tensions which stop his own
progress. Sue complements Jude's ambivalence and their aborted

union reflects a predicament of moral restlessness. Neither seems able to maintain an integrity of purpose amidst the exigencies of a changing world, and in this sense they are comparable to the Idiot archetype in their weak and ineffective intransigence. They have not sufficiently made the adjustment to the new alignment and yet falter in their convictions of an older creed. What becomes characteristic of them is what Hardy terms 'the modern vice of unrest' (98) which typifies their moral crisis. At no point do they achieve a sense of peace and complacency.

The novel is structured by a series of predicaments that are symptomatic of Decadence. It burgeons in the perverse and paradoxical turn of events which prevent the lawful union of Sue and Jude despite their definite attraction for each other and their marked similarity of comportment. This sustained tension, unresolvable, impedes the creation of climax in the novel. Instead, recurring and episodic patterns of reunion and separation occur at various junctions in the narrative as the two chief characters intermittently establish unsatisfactory relationships outside their 'illegal' but affective bond. It is seen how Jude inappropriately allies himself with Arabella, though he does not savour what Hardy calls her 'crudity'. And Sue marries the prosaic Phillotson, whose apparent stability will not calm her perennial restlessness. Hardy communicates the snags and strains of action along a whole topography of furze and pickets which trace his characters' jagged moral peregrinations.

As this succession of stalemate situations characterizes the narrative, expressed most poignantly in the thwarted relationship of Sue and Jude, a case of Jamesian postponement of action can be identified. This is first expressed in terms of a certain sexual reticence. One particular instance occurs when Sue and Jude are reunited after Sue separates from Phillotson with his consent. At that point, Jude arranges for a single room at the Temperance Hotel, and Sue hedges at the thought of such intimacy, fearing compromise. To give herself physically to Jude would be an emotional commitment which she is not prepared to enact: 'Put it down to my timidity . . . to a woman's natural timidity when the crisis comes' (287–8). The thought of such intimacy with Jude creates in her a sense of crisis, and it is only Arabella's sudden appearance on the scene, inciting jealousy and actual threat, which moves the action at that point. Sue's major weakness is her inability to act, demonstrated in her reluctance to make an outright commitment to Jude or to move impulsively without rational justification. In this respect, her character is similar to James's Isabel Archer and has similar effects upon the plot. A certain hesitancy to fulfil her desires is evidenced in her guarded relationship with Jude, a rapport that is marked by a fastidiousness and self-consciousness. In this manner, she shares Jude's 'ratiocinative meditativeness' and, as Phillotson rightly notes, the two cousins are two of a kind as they suffer from a similar atrophy in dealing with practical matters.

The crisis is drawn out to a point where a marriage between the two is agreed upon but not enacted. The principle of postponement affects this stage of the narrative: 'They thought it over, or postponed thinking. Certainly they postponed action, and seemed to love on in a dream paradise' (328). At this crucial point, they both renegue, unable to circumscribe in a binding social and material contract the 'volatile essence' (338). It becomes clear that the perverse sensitivities of Sue and Jude make them falter and debilitate the action. Sue is a vessel of emotion and recognizes this as an ailment which also afflicts Jude: 'we are a weak, tremulous pair, Jude' (344). Jude attributes their failure at commitment to this excess of emotion: 'We are horribly sensitive; that's really what's the matter with us, Sue!' (345). This perverse sensitivity can be envisaged as a sign of the Decadent quality of their personalities. Their constant deliberation of thought and feeling puts them in a position of non-participation and non-commitment as illustrated in the way they passively observe a marriage ceremony before them instead of actively uniting in a legal marriage themselves. Sue's generalization of their particular case into a contagious crisis syndrome, eschatological in its effects on the destiny of the human race, becomes one of the most portentous and morbid statements of the novel:

> Everybody is getting to feel as we do. We are a little beforehand, that's all. In fifty, a hundred years the descent of these two will act and feel worse than we. They will see weltering humanity still more vividly than we do now, as 'Shapes like our own selves hideously multiplied', and will be afraid to reproduce them. (345)

Mrs Edlin, the provincial gauge of the past, corroborates Sue's fears, as she later remarks in her natural idiom how complex matrimonial commitment has become: 'one really do feel *afeard to move* in it at all' (444).

Undirected, then, their emotion becomes diluted and frustrated through the rest of the novel, as the lovers are drawn back to their legal mates and their lives are unhappily separated as they forfeit their aspirations for love. What becomes apparent is the ineffectuality of love to endure the harsher forces of reality which Arabella and Phillotson represent in their respective sectors. Along with the ineffectiveness of metaphysics and theology is the crisis and weakening of the greatest of spiritual factors in the Western erotic tradition. Whereas the novel *Tess of the d'Urbervilles* had demonstrated failure of love in the context of Romance, *Jude the Obscure* casts such failure in terms of Realism, thereby making this observation all the more devastating.

Hardy communicates this spiritual malady through the structural web of crisis circumstances which recur and become a recognizable pattern in his fiction. Particularly in *Jude the Obscure*, Hardy conceives the intricate web of flawed human relationships as a focus for modernism, even as James. Repeatedly, and almost obsessively, he charts the estrangements between the two pairs of characters as a recurring pattern in the fragile rapports. This repetition turns what would appear as a single crisis into a chronic one. Furthermore, in their recurrence, the stagnant situations begin to be identified as natural states rather than as exceptional cases. Hardy presents a series of mismatches, and his characters' search for appropriate mates seems to be a futile one. A regressive pattern in the plot is the outcome of his last novel, as Phillotson returns to Marygreen with Sue, and Jude is found again in the cottage outside Christminster with Arabella. The 'belaboured progress' of the novel ironically culminates in the definite halt of its most symptomatic character, Jude.

Certainly, of the three novels, *Jude the Obscure* becomes the most static as it emphasizes through Jude's personal problematics the toll taken by the chronic crisis syndrome. The novel seems to exude a brooding atmosphere of ponderous perplexity from which the principal character cannot liberate himself; so suffocated is he that he believes 'to be born is a palpable dilemma'. Jude's state of mind seems to be the vehicle for communicating this 'modern' mental condition. His behaviour becomes a predictable pose of meditativeness. The novel's action seems subservient to the identification of the 'Jude' condition from various vantage points with disturbing frequency.

The particulars of Jude's existence, his frustrated aspirations for religious and intellectual ideals, his metaphysical orphanage, his failure in amorous relationships, extend beyond his class structure as aspects of the human condition at the advent of the modern world. At times, he can be associated with the Idiot, even though the gap in social station between the two types is immense. That Christianity and Western learning are inaccessible to him proves their ineffectuality in a world which is producing the realities of an Arabella's animality and of a Father Time's post-decadence. The last image of Jude as 'a 'andsome corpse', to use Arabella's words, lying amidst old superseded editions of Virgil and Horace and a dog-eared Greek Testament, indicates dire futility. The books of Christminster, in deteriorated and dusty state, suggest a Faust-like study which is lifeless and ineffectual, and demonstrate the jeopardy haunting Western Gothic man.

Hardy becomes a true moralizer of declines and falls as he examines in his most memorable characters the atrophy and paralysis caused by the 'ache of modernism' and adjusts his narrative to the 'new alignment'. In his novels, he defines the 'modern' ailment as the pensive turmoil which he sees as having developed in reaction to the changing physical and metaphysical environment. He exposes his characters to the pressures of an exigent materialism created by the social, biological and political advances of the epoch. Those who can be considered 'decadent' types, sociologically and historically, appear as a variety of extinct species lacking the energy and will to engage in the Darwinian struggle for survival and advancement. Such characters are raised from their local perspectives and depicted as problematic identities, culminating in the most disturbing of complexities of Jude Fawley and Sue Bridehead, as has been seen. These two are markedly trapped in the rarefied atmosphere of the crisis situation and vacillate in unresolvable dilemmas between two worlds and value systems. From this later novel emerges most noticeably a characteristically Decadent structure of the Hardy narrative in its chronic repetition.

Of the novelists considered here, Hardy best expresses Decadence in a metaphysical context, ultimately viewing it in terms of human dislocation. It has been seen how his Decadent characters seem out of joint and tragic in their struggle with an imposing environment. Their status in the universe, as well as in society, is a marginal one. Their moral stamina weakens consistently, as if by a spiritual disease. Hardy's expression is one broad pastiche of nebulous identities, both morally and socially, ever yearning for completion yet consistently and chronically frustrated in that reaching. An atmosphere of Decadence is conveyed through images of the physical rottenness of stone, of waning, of crumbling, of draining and extinction. The obscurity of the characters in the light of such an environment is a sign of their modernity, foreshadowing complete character breakdown which was to predominate in fiction after the turn of the century. The stalemate of action breaks normative narrative flow from crisis to resolution. In the waning years of the nineteenth century, Hardy caught and prolonged the crisis moments of that foreshadowing.

6 Joseph Conrad and the Dissolution of an Ethical Code: the Hollow Centre

Conrad possessed what could be considered the most fully integrated of 'Western eyes'. His Polish origin, his sojourn in France and adopted British citizenship (in 1886), his perspective of voyage did endow him with a cosmopolitan status[1] which was well adapted to a critical assessment of an entire cultural condition. In fact, he insisted on his Western European identity: 'Western Roman culture derived at first from Italy and then from France',[2] he explained. Like Hardy and Dostoevsky, he presaged with pessimism an incipient avalanche over Europe. But as a writer deploring the distortions of imperialism, his target of attack was not only politics but language and in particular the conventional *word*. He declared this emphatically in the celebrated preface to *The Nigger of the 'Narcissus'*: 'old, old words, worn thin, defaced by ages of careless usage.'[3]

That T. S. Eliot was to encapsulate his poetic statement on the decline of Western civilization[4] with an epigraph drawn from *Heart of Darkness* (1899), 'Mistah Kurtz – he dead', suggests that Conrad's expression of decadence is indeed mythic and cultural. Eliot's 'hollow men' do reverberate the Kurtz-like turn-of-the-century Western men of Conrad. And the moribund figure of Kurtz among all Conrad's figures, and for that matter above all modern figures, looms like a sign, a portent and paradoxically an embodiment of lost significance. It is a fact that the reader never gets to know Kurtz, and this intentional ambiguity concerning the personality of the figure substitutes in the place of a psychological authenticity a mythical one. Compelling as Hardy in the creation of the Jude figure, Conrad proceeded to construct and deconstruct a momentous cultural conglomerate: 'All Europe contributed to the making of Kurtz' (117). In a single phrase or in a few stark words, Conrad was able to transmit his dread of the ineffectuality of an entire culture, as the word 'horror', onomatopoeic in effect, had the potency of a resonant presagement. Predating Freud and Spengler, he seems to be one of the first to challenge the concept of civilization, attributing a derogatory implication to the notion of culture. Looking with anguish at what he discerned to be the fate of Western man 'in the flicker', Conrad paradoxically created a character embodying moral dissolution symptomatic of Decadence.

Conrad first envisaged such deterioration in terms of politicized Western colonial jargon, remarking ironically through the very title 'An Outpost of Progress':

Everybody shows a respectful deference to certain sounds that he and his fellows can make. But about feelings people really know nothing. We talk with indignation or enthusiasm; we talk about oppression, cruelty, crime, devotion, self-sacrifice, virtue, and we know nothing beyond the words. (105)

Attrition and misuse with the tide of time seem to have destroyed the effectiveness of such language, thereby necessitating the creation of a new vocabulary along with a new secular–ethical code. Interestingly, Conrad's complaint here seems to echo a Zarathustra-like reckoning with what Nietzsche had called 'noble words'. It is here directed specifically against the language of humanitarian self-righteousness and benevolence which flourished in the heyday of the New Imperialism of the 1880s and 1890s. It also anticipates in a later context the fervour of George Orwell's attack on meaningless rhetoric in his famous essay 'Politics and the English Language'.

In this perspective of imminent decay, it was Conrad's intent to revive language from its graveyard of dead images and worn words, sensitive as he was to the aging process which he had detected within his cultural vistas. For this purpose, he amalgamates the poetic and cultural trends of the time and the scrutiny of language conducted by such writers as Flaubert, Mallarmé[5] and the Symbolists. In a similar way to that of the writers here considered, Conrad transcribes the thematics of Decadence into symbolist prose. He casts a 'magic suggestiveness' over the erosion he perceives. Moreover, from the monad of the word, Conrad proceeds to focus on the narrative structure of the tale. Here this is the yarn of the seaman, whose chief spokesman becomes his Buddha-like persona-narrator, Marlow, unravelling the tale and grappling with the centre:

> But Marlow was not typical (if his propensity to spin yarns be excepted), and to him the meaning of an episode was not inside like a kernel but outside, enveloping the tale which brought it out only as a glow brings out a haze, in the likeness of one of these misty halos that sometimes are made visible by the spectral illumination of moonshine. (48)

When Conrad arrived at the construction of the work *Heart of Darkness*, he was to associate most fully the moral crises he had been observing with a literary shift. The distancing from the centre, the delay to the climax, the suspending quality of the visual image, the fragmentation into metonymy convey in process the displacement of Western moral significance.

The cluster of stories prior and inferior to *Heart of Darkness* represents not only an 1890s mood, as is the case particularly of *Almayer's Folly*, but also adumbrations and trials which lead to the decentred novella, *Heart of Darkness*. This group includes such Malayan tales as *Almayer's Folly* (1895), *An Outcast of the Islands* (1896), *The Nigger of the 'Narcissus'* (1897), 'Youth' (1898) and the African 'An Outpost of Progress' (1898), specifically anticipating *Heart of Darkness*. It can be seen how the literal character portrayal and structural design of these early works provide the background for the symbolization that obtains in the well wrought *Heart of Darkness*. At the very turn of the century, Conrad was to intensify and condense his expression of Decadence.

It has been noted, for example, that *Almayer's Folly*, dealing as it does with a defeated Dutch colonialist, conveys in particular the weariness of *fin-de-siècle* writings through the prevalent presence of fatigue. Some critics have gone so far as to assert that Almayer is like the century itself, ready to expire. In depicting a failed colonialist-trader in Borneo, living in a fast-decaying, partially-constructed house which was to be the house of his dreams, the story presents in a very overt manner an atmosphere of decline with respect to a twenty-year colonial adventure. A Kurtz-like figure is intimated both by Almayer himself, who in his greed for gold harbours dreams of mansions and wealth in Amsterdam, and by the absent Captain Lingard, the formidable trading manager for whose favour Almayer sells himself out. Almayer's schemes are ruined by the abandonment of Lingard (who himself has been bankrupt), by the natives and in particular by the plot of his Sulu wife. For she recognizes that his marriage to her had been to please the manager and become heir to his fortune. His trading mission fails miserably and Almayer succumbs to death at the end of this story, debilitated by a weariness and overwhelming fatigue which contribute to his downfall and collapse. Aside from a few images relating to the actual decay of Almayer's 'house of ambition' and a general brownish atmosphere in the setting, the story pronounces this condition rather than suggests it. That it is composed in preparation for *Heart of Darkness*, however, is substantiated by the fact that it was written during the first stages of Conrad's Congo journey – while he was reaping impressions for the subsequent novella.

In gathering the symptoms of Decadence, Conrad proceeds from fatigue to surrender and paralysis, as it will be seen. As many critics have noted, the focus is upon the weakening of the will. In the case of the story, *An Outcast of the Islands*, perhaps even the name of the principal character suggests this fact. That Willems's amorous affair with the Arab girl, Aissa, has implications beyond a romantic love affair is particularly apparent in the way he contemplates his sexual surrender. He envisages it reflexively as the yielding of the soul to the unconscious forces of the greater self: 'He looked into that great dark place odorous with the breath of life, with the mystery of existence, renewed, fecund, indestructible; and he felt afraid . . . in the presence of his unconscious and ardent struggle' (337). Here it is the darkness of the night which contains that paradoxical, destructive fecundity associated in other works with the sea and most potently, of course, with the darkness of the heart of the African jungle. Willems, a characteristically Conradian character, distinctly views his surrender to the forces of the wilderness as an act of decline and personal perdition: 'the deliberate descent from his pedestal, the throwing away of his superiority, of all his hopes, of old ambitions, of the ungrateful civilization' (337). His status as an outcast for his betrayal of his patron Hudig is compounded by his conscious and vindictive yielding of 'civilization' to 'savagery', conceptually speaking. The 'relaxation of his muscles' metaphorically implies the dissolution of his personal integrity, as Conrad develops the symbolic components of his expression of sexual love. This is emphasized particularly in Willems's subsequent association of defunct images with his passion and his self-characterization as a 'lost man'. The notion of hollowness is especially descriptive of that loss: 'And, all at once, it seemed to him that he was peering into a sombre *hollow*, into a deep black hole full of *decay* and of whitened bones' (339). This eschatological sense, derived from what would seem at first reading a 'mere' act of passion is prolonged by the use of such superlative words as 'cataclysm', 'paralysing awe', 'disaster', 'destruction', which terminate the story and lead to the murder of the debilitated hero by the 'destructive element' which Aissa represents.

It is also interesting to notice Conrad's lexicon in identifying Willems's moral perversion at the beginning of the novel as an 'excursion into the wayside quagmires', and a 'sentence in brackets' (3). This excursion from the moral path (referring first specifically to Willems's appropriation of Hudig's money) is a first deviation from a linear pattern – remindful as well of Hardy, for the 'quagmire' suggests a perplexity which ensues. This terminology turns a marginal perspective into a central one – enacting a structural displacement which becomes much more significant stylistically in *Heart of Darkness*.

In both *Almayer's Folly* and *An Outcast of the Islands*, it is also true that amidst Conrad's indulgently overstated descriptions of exotic landscapes, which seem to be spontaneous impressions of his Bornean adventures, Decadent motifs emerge from recurring images. The languor of the landscape permeates the characters. The many streams and drifting dead barks floating down passively into darkness become objective equivalents of the process of the surrender of the will to wild and primitive forces. Descriptions of such streams are found both at the beginning of *Almayer's Folly* and toward the end of *An Outcast of the Islands*. Almayer's attention, for example, at the beginning is captured by the fate of a drifting tree amidst the violence of a brutal river, and this reminds him of his own passivity and failure. In general these images appear to allude to the fate of the weakened heroes who betray their duties and loyalties through the weakness of the will. These streams in Sambir ultimately culminate into the Thames and Congo rivers: mental passageways lead into the 'heart of an immense darkness', where Conrad detects a paralysed soul.

Most significant among his early works, however, is *The Nigger of the 'Narcissus'*, which contains germs of *Heart of Darkness* and which serves as an experimental path to it as the Decadent factor begins to infect Conrad's prose. Though traditional in its narrative structure of a sea adventure story and based on a personal voyage that Conrad had actually taken in Bombay in 1884, the steady realistic sequence of the narrative is disrupted by characters who become personifications of the death process and a formal factor in the de-knotting of the plot. The ship, though realistically called the *Narcissus*, becomes the vehicle for a metaphysical journey, a kind of *bateau ivre* detached from the earth – a voyage of the unconscious self. The preface to the work also indicates that something portentous was happening in this tale as Conrad envisaged his art in terms of the symbolic usage of the 'rescued fragment'.

The story, perhaps better known by Conrad's celebrated preface to it on his aesthetics, relates an episode whereby a newly-formed crew of an English merchant ship returning from the Far East experiences near-shipwreck while being under the influence of a single member, the black James Wait, who is dying in their midst. At times it is ambiguous whether his state is authentic or sham, but when in the course of the turbulent voyage he becomes entrapped in his cabin, the crew scrambles to rescue him in a concerted effort to stalk the foreboding powers of death. The moribund figure brings out the anarchic forces of the crew. When the captain finally bans Wait from duty, the crew nearly mutinies. They return to shore and separate, perhaps wiser but sadder mariners who are alienated after a voyage of existential experience that has threatened their moral security.

The disruption of the crew and their moral weakening under the influence of Wait is contrasted with the ethical code represented and upheld by the venerable old seaman, Singleton. Singleton is described as being strong, selfless, courageous and 'unthinking': a true man of the sea who had 'never given a thought to his mortal self' (99). Like Hardy, Conrad seems to be associating decadence with the new generation of Western men, here identified with the younger crewmen who are characterized as a 'crowd of softies' with 'sentimental voices' (25). At the beginning of the novel, he refers to Singleton as 'a lonely relic of a

devoured and forgotten generation' (24) in contrast with his
successors, who are 'the grown-up children of a discontented
earth' (25). In this light, the wallowing in moral incertitude which
besets the crew in the course of the voyage is symptomatic of the
process whereby modern men have become orphans once again,
metaphysically speaking. The mention of the 'grown-up' children
echoes Hardy's perceptions of the modern types. The perplexity
and fear which comprise the Decadence of the crew members
pertains to a greater moral ambiguity existing beyond the
confines of this single, emblematic voyage. It extends to the
collective, aged, eschatological condition of Western men, which
Conrad subsequently highlighted in his story 'Youth': 'lined',
'wrinkled', 'tired men from the West sleeping . . . in careless
attitudes of death' (41–2). The sea, characteristically for Conrad,
remains the forum for the aloof universe. In *The Nigger of the
'Narcissus'*, Singleton, in his strict adherence to duty and toil,
remains emotionally and intellectually immune from the recognition of that indifference and from the debilitating effects of the
character Wait.

Much of the novel focuses upon the particular effects which
Wait has upon the Narcissus crew, a crew composed of men of
variegated Western extraction, except for Wait. He first appears
as the last of the eighteen crewmen to enlist on the voyage and is
pictured as a lean figure standing ominously against a rail. Much
of Wait's effect is atmospheric, as he is initially described
exhuming a mist of darkness around him. Often heard gasping for
breath or coughing, he has a voice that rings 'hollow and loud'
(35). His presence on the ship paradoxically combines fragility
and force as he pridefully parades his dying body, intimidating
the crew and interfering with their activities. The first evidence of
their progressive moral breakdown is when they begin to steal pie
and food provisions from the cook to feed Wait surreptitiously.

It is as if the principal character, Wait, though in this case *not*
Western[6], serves as the skin of darkness (in this story) from which
Conrad proceeds to examine the core (in *Heart of Darkness*). And
the empty core which was to become obvious in the case of Kurtz
carries trappings of the lethal, deteriorating skin examined in *The
Nigger of the 'Narcissus'*. Wait eventually immobilizes and paralyses
the crew, which becomes unusually subservient to this symbol
of stalking death before them. In a transparent way, they
succumb in pity and fear to the destructive element. It is upon

their weakening and demise that Conrad focuses in this story, which evokes a morbid image – an image which seems later to be appropriated by T. S. Eliot in his poetic conception of the 'hollow men':

> We are the hollow men
> We are the stuffed men
> Leaning together
> Headpiece filled with straw . . .[7]

Here is Conrad's initial version: 'he was only a cold black skin loosely stuffed with soft cotton wool; his arms and legs swung jointless and pliable; his head rolled about; the lower lip hung down, enormous and heavy' (71). Wait resembles an effigy, as does the figure of Guy Fawkes alluded to by Eliot. All toil is terminated as the paralysed crew remains stupefied in the presence of Wait and falls victim to anarchic forces unleashed by death. As in the case of Eliot, the greatest debilitating agent is death itself, which decimates moral stamina and courage.

Conrad actually and literally conceives of this character as a demoralizing element among civilized men and 'decadence' specifically becomes the word he chooses to describe this process of mollification: 'He was demoralizing. Through him we were becoming highly humanized, tender, complex, excessively *decadent*' (139) (emphasis added). It is interesting to scrutinize the words that Conrad uses to describe the effects of weakening: the word 'tender' makes of this fear a sensual experience. An effeminite mellowing is produced which Conrad identifies earlier in the text as a kind of 'sentimentality' and which he distinguishes from moral and courageous vigour. It also is comparable to the 'sweet' surrender in an act of love. Here, however, it implies an awakened sensitivity or consciousness. This increasing egoism is accompanied by a growing sense of anxiety which Conrad expresses in terms of the crew's concern over Wait: 'the latent egoism of tenderness to suffering appeared in the developing anxiety not to see him die' (138). Wait gains an imperious control over their souls: 'We made a chorus of affirmation to his wildest assertions. . . . He influenced *the moral tone of our world*' (139) (emphasis added). The crew views itself as being 'overcivilized and rotten' (139) – which here implies an over-ripeness of certain faculties. Conrad is depicting the state of excessive reflectiveness which characterizes the 'decadents', common among advanced stages of civilization, as Thomas Hardy had previously noted.[8] In a letter to his friend R. B. Cunninghame Graham in 1898, Conrad himself later generalizes: 'What makes mankind tragic is not that they are the victims of nature, it is that they are conscious of it.'[9] The 'sentimentality' produced by the egocentric awareness of the absurd condition derives not from the condition itself, but from the growing consciousness of it. Were Conrad simply depicting the depravity, it would be a Naturalistic portrait. The awareness of the weakness is a form of negative narcissism and this obsessive consciousness makes the study a portrait of Decadence.

Like Henry James, Conrad enacts in the narrative a 'decadent' postponement of death through the figure of Wait (even suggested in his name) who 'too long delayed to die' (145). The ship is regarded as a silent purveyor of death as it and the narrative steadily lose their realistic character and become remembered as a 'shadowy ship manned by a crew of Shades' (173). Under the influence of Wait the crew of Western men appears as silhouettes: Conrad has graphically depicted not only the surrender of the will to amorphous shapes and postures but character-evisceration as well. When Wait eventually dies as the ship approaches the shore, the ending is achieved, as its postponement runs out. Furthermore, a 'disengaged' narrator emerges, soon to become Marlow.

In creating James Wait, Conrad has here isolated a central figure which incarnates the demoralizing factor, thereby using character as symbolic personification of moral vacuity. Already in *The Nigger of the 'Narcissus'*, then, he had created an 'empty man', '-empty-empty' (113), he repeats. The next step was Kurtz and the hollow centre. Both the names, Kurtz and Wait, suggest reduced value or dehumanized significance. Both figures emit hollow and loud metallic voices in their death rattles. If Wait is the living emblem of death, it is ultimately Kurtz, ivory not black, who is made into a colossal immorality.

The much-discussed *Heart of Darkness* reverberates with multiple interpretations from the hollow core that is Kurtz. The reader is deftly led by the questing narrator Marlow (acquired in the short story 'Youth') to the character in the inner station whose moral make-up lies at the surface of the reverberating word. The narrative technique of frames involves the telling of a tale through a series of impressions, anticipations, hearsay, visualizations and adumbrations. When the narrator ultimately reaches the protaganist, he approaches the discourse which conveys the man through the ominous word 'horror', whose meaning is communicated through its effect. In the case of Conrad, the spatial forms are not those of a moral maze, as in the case of Thomas Hardy, but rather of a vacuous centre which has surrendered significance to the shells of envelopment and to the repercussions of the surface sound of words.

The setting sun, the gloomy haze of the Thames river poeticize the cultural perspective with which the West is critically envisaged at the onset of the novel and foreshadow the appearance of the Kurtz figure much later in the novel. The first few pages simulate in masterly fashion the slow motions of the sinking sun and render a poetics of decline. Conrad, this last writer under consideration, in 1899, presents a most fitting natural correlative of decline, conveying both the beauty and the tedious prolongation of such a fall:

> The day was ending in a serenity of still and exquisite brilliance. . . . And at last, in its curved and imperceptible fall, the sun sank low, and from glowing white changed to a dull red without rays and without heat, as if about to go out suddenly stricken to death by the touch of that gloom brooding over a crowd of men. (46)

The aging condition of the British empire is stressed in reference to the old Thames river and the abiding memories of conquest it harbours (from Sir Francis Drake onwards). This atmospheric prologue is connected to the main body of the work by the very image of the Thames river 'stretched before us like the beginning of an interminable waterway' (45), the stream of consciousness that will lead the narrator on his physical and metaphysical journey to the Congo river.

From the beginning, Conrad ironically envisages the emissaries of 'civilization' betrayed by the past dreams of conquest: 'the dreams of men, the seed of commonwealths, the germs of empires' (47) and more modern-day justifications of 'efficiency' and 'idea' as popularized by Kipling and his contemporaries. In a letter to his publisher William Blackwood in 1898, Conrad describes his forthcoming novel as exposing the 'criminality of inefficiency and pure selfishness'.[10] His critique of imperialism was to be harboured in the Kurtz figure, who paradoxically represents the lights of 'progress', 'pity' and 'science' in the heart of darkness.

The consciousness of the narrator Marlow steadily grows as he recounts the approach to the centre to the crew of the *Nellie*, anchored on the Thames. Marlow conducts a steady and determined search for a truth, both cultural and metaphysical, and he knows that the process of the narrative will unveil it. So too does the listener, presumably Conrad: 'I listened, I listened on the watch for the sentence, for the word, that would give me the clue to the faint uneasiness inspired by this narrative that seemed to shape itself without human lips in the heavy night-air of the river' (83). The unravelling of the tale occurs through a process likened to the musical effects of dream, proceeding by powers of association and arresting image-making.

The approach to Kurtz, who contains the telling word at the core of the narrative, is delayed, and this forestallment with respect to the underlying truth resembles the deferment technically enacted in Jamesian prose. As the narrator, here a consciously identified one, recounts the slow but steady passageway from the outposts to the central station, he continues in the narrative the thematics of decline foreshadowed by the atmospheric effects of the opening pages. Marlow relates how he initially gets a position of captain of a large trading company ship by replacing a Dane, called Fresleven, who had succumbed to an act of futile violence in a quarrel over two black hens. The lack of proportion and the incongruity between the Dane's death and the cause for the quarrel, ironically viewed in the rubric of the 'noble cause', are the first of a set of absurd and horrific behavioural patterns within the African setting. They also ironically point to the deterioration of the imperialistic code in the alien environment.

Marlow describes his first encounter with the natives at the company's station as an 'inferno' scene. It is indeed Dantesque in its depiction of death and human attrition in sensual and concrete forms. The landscape is composed of dark shapes and forms as the narrator can only identify 'black shadows of disease', 'dark things' and 'moribund shapes' in a 'greenish gloom'. His impression is marked by an accumulation of such images which paraphrase the human element. The narrator recognizes the humans through bodily parts of bones, eyelids, necks, ribs, joints. These metonymies highlight the dehumanization which he witnesses, and in revealing them he conducts a deconstruction of human form. Eventually the shapes are reduced to postures of crouching or contorted collapse, and facial expressions of startling vacancy as in the instance: 'The black bones reclined at full length with one shoulder against the tree, and slowly the eyelids rose and the sunken eyes looked up at me, enormous and vacant, a kind of blind, white flicker in the depths of the orbs, which died out slowly' (66). The lethal gaze has the eschatological dimension of Rogozhin's eyes in Dostoevsky's *Idiot* – which functions also in that context as a challenge to integrity and promotes a vision of fragmentation, as has been seen. Conrad's most vivid example of the reduction of the human element is the following observation: 'Near the same tree two more bundles of acute angles sat with their legs drawn up' (67). What is striking is the vivid description of moral vacancy in terms of shape, colour and form, as registered in this scene of strong sensory effect. Decay and death occupy a principal role in the novella from this scene on.

The progressive probing inward is conveyed in Marlow's account of his movement from the central to the inner station, wherein lies the prodigious Kurtz. Along the way, Marlow encounters inhumanity in the person of the well-groomed accountant who is insensitive to the moanings around him. He sees decaying machinery of an uncompleted and abandoned railway as a sham of the forces of 'progress'. He considers the Eldorado Exploring Expedition, which suddenly appears before him, as a travesty of purpose. But as Marlow journeys on the steamer to the interior of the jungle, the earth loses all semblance of reality for him, and he seems enveloped as if in a dream. Marlow becomes progressively alienated from his surroundings, as threats of cannibalism by the pilgrims on the steamer confront him. He begins to ponder the meaning of the word 'restraint' in such a setting, identifying the quality which he will discover the enigmatic Kurtz had abandoned in the gratification of his unwieldy lust. The word 'flabby' will be associated, as it was in Zola's imagination, with the loss of self-control and with that factor of excess viewed as decadent.

The signal which prefigures Kurtz are the heads on the tops of stakes in the vicinity of the dwelling. Marlow's steamer is beckoned to shore by Kurtz's last disciple, a young Russian. The atmosphere becomes increasingly nightmarish, as the Russian resembles a harlequin dressed in motley and a general sense of madness pervades the area. The scene is marked by a kind of Dionysian aura as 'wild glances' and 'savage movements', shrill cries and colourful costumes characterize the sensual landscape. Horned heads, painted faces, scarlet bodies appear before Marlow. The motions are subsequently interpreted as funeral rites, a dance of death for the dying Kurtz. This vivid eschatological imagery prepares Marlow for the vision of Kurtz, who is brought out on the stretcher before him. This atmosphere which suggests a subconscious topography is appropriate to the contemplation of the 'horror' of the 'hollow man'.

Marlow is given his last secondary account of Kurtz through the Russian who seems to confirm all the hearsay he has already acquired. The Russian ardently comments, in impressionable phrases, upon the prodigious effect which Kurtz has had upon him: 'this man has enlarged my mind' (125) with his eloquent talks on love, justice and conduct. 'They adored him' (128), he remarks in reference to the natives who had idolized him. But as Marlow finally sees Kurtz, he finds that a kind of Nemesis had overtaken the former raider and pillager, who himself had been invaded by the greater wilderness. His ascendance has been checked, as he lies helplessly dying upon a stretcher. The original Kurtz has been reduced to a 'hollow sham' (147) and the narrative presents the most colossal and dramatic Decadent of all.

What Marlow ultimately encounters in the presence of Kurtz is a voice and an expression. As in the case of Hardy and of Dostoevsky, Conrad focuses upon a visage, a facial expression, as being representative of the condition of Western man: 'that ivory face the expression of sombre pride, or ruthless power, of craven terror – of an intense and hopeless despair' (149). It is to be remembered that Conrad makes of Kurtz a cultural prodigy, gifted in art, music, rhetoric and poetry, so that in his deteriorated condition he becomes a product of Western civilization.

Marlow's confrontation with the character Kurtz occurs almost anticlimactically, after he has undergone the trials and tribulations of his journey, which becomes the rite of passage. The 'adjectival vagueness' used to describe Kurtz, as a long, indistinct and vaporous figure, corresponds to the moral ambiguity of the character's make-up. Soon surfaces vanish, as the narrator comes face to face with *the* heart of darkness and perilously close to his own extinction. Through Marlow, the reader is drawn to the dead centre, and the contact with that centre is a supreme moment of literary experience. The words of Kurtz to Marlow lose their denotative significance and acquire a connotative one of suggestiveness:

> They were common everyday words – the familiar vague sounds exchanged on every waking day of life. But what of that? They had behind them to my mind, the terrific suggestiveness of words heard in dreams, of phrases spoken in nightmare. Soul! If anybody ever struggled with a soul, I am the man. (144)

Ironically, Marlow comments that no eloquence would have been as devastating as Kurtz's 'final burst of sincerity': 'the horror'. It is as if he were in the presence of a modern-day Faust who, having surrendered his soul to a morally vacant self, communicates the savage truth he had discovered about the human condition.

Paradoxically, Kurtz's curt and abbreviated expression, transmitted by a whisper, hyperbolizes the message he carries regarding the naked and futile state of man at the core. His own very existence is a hyperbole of solipsism, reminiscent of the 'Narcissus' case, as Marlow witnesses his self-adulation. As an individual, Kurtz becomes a paradox of 'exalted degradation'. In all his apparent force, he manifests his Decadence by being morally impotent. An 'immense emptiness of darkness' himself, he incarnates a hyperbole as large and unnatural as the flower of Mallarmé or Huysmans or the dark and voracious mine of Zola representing the excess associated with Decadence in this study. He is a symbol of extreme and misguided individuality.

Conrad has aptly chosen the name of Kurtz for its German meaning of 'brief' – to represent the multinational synthesis of all Europeans. Here the Decadence approaches the level of myth as it is crystallized collectively in the individual character of Kurtz, who represents not only England but Western society at large. This justifies giving a foreign name to the principal character. Furthermore, it becomes apparent that Kurtz may well be an ironic synonym for Faust.[11] The outright failure of Western man to live up to the principles and ideals traditionally held by the imperial societies which produced him has the element of the perverse. Kurtz's attested insensitivity to those ideals and to the responsibilities of the 'white man's burden' can be likened to a void created by the malfunctioning of a life-sustaining organ.

The final image of the waning, diseased Kurtz, wrapped in a

sheet, could be said to reflect the moral decay of his European society, and once again in this narrative structured upon the dimensions of Decadence, the central character is symptomatic of the society which produced him. The imprint on his face is the frightful pallor of the ivory which he has rapaciously pursued in his acts of avarice and brutality. In contrast to the lethal forms around him, his is a greater darkness of blank vacuity, and Kurtz looms as the most colossal figure of cultural decadence of all the ones considered heretofore.

The centre of the narrative, hence, contains a moribund specimen with a hollow core. The narrator, Marlow, enacts the decentring of narrative, which results from his slow approach to and immediate withdrawal from the empty centre. It is true that Marlow himself risks annihilation in this 'sickly atmosphere of tepid scepticism', but the solipsistic disease is not contagious because Marlow's concern is elsewhere, as he proceeds out from the centre. Marlow has not only witnessed a spectacular instance of human degradation in his encounter with Kurtz, but he has also encountered the deteriorated figure of meaning. His experience is comparable with the phenomenon in Jamesian prose whereby elements of narrative are made visceral and material. This effect is here achieved by the visible annihilation of the central character.

A moral experience has dramatically affected the structure of plot. The climax is attenuated as Marlow flees in shock and terror, having reaped the word best fit to express the experience. It is as if the narrator Marlow returns to the sepulchral city in Belgium, equipped with the seeds of Decadent narrative. Ready to perpetrate the 'lie' or artifice in his rendition of the tale, he actually manipulates the plot and embraces the aesthetic alternative as he confronts the faithful Muse or Kurtz's Intended or saving illusion.

A distancing has occurred whereby Marlow has depersonalized the experience through the act of interpretation. As a mediator, he proceeds to veil the grim and abominable reality of the social decadence he has witnessed along with the absurdity inherent in the Naturalistic vision. Like Hardy and Zola before him, Conrad transcends the dark substratum through the process of art. Attention is drawn toward Marlow's detachment from the destructive experience, as he sacrifices the ruinous sincerity of a Kurtz for constructive dissimulation, the technical metamorphosis being the outcome of the moral demise. It is as if Conrad were combining an aesthetic manifesto with a moral tract, justifying Oscar Wilde's thesis of the 'decay of lying' by an acceptance of a decadent state of civilization. Although Marlow himself remarks at one point that he hates lies because there is 'a taint of death, a flavour of mortality' (94) in them, he none the less suggests that maintaining them is the only refuge from the consciousness which he has painfully acquired of the neutral universe.

It is known how appalled Conrad himself was with the notion of the indifferent universe. With the fortifying attitude of ironic jest, he made the final 'naturalistic' conjecture of the century in both eschatological and phantasmagoric terms. The background for the novella had been drawn in 1897 in a letter. The terms are as vividly haunting and apocalyptic as Dostoevsky's tarantula image (rendered by the character Ippolit) or Zola's bestial portrait of the consuming mine:

> There is a, – let us say, – a machine. It evolved itself (I am severely scientific) out of a chaos of scraps of iron and behold! – it knits. I am horrified at the horrible work and stand appalled. I feel it ought to embroider, – but it goes on knitting. You come and say: 'This is all right: it's only a question of the right kind of oil. Let us use this, – for instance, – celestial oil and the machine will embroider a most beautiful design in purple and gold.'[12]

It is interesting that the mention of purple and gold conjures the association of Symbolist art with the end of Empire which the poet Verlaine had communicated in his poem 'Langueur' and its 'style d'or' (golden style). In that context it had been a question of the end of Second Empire France with associations of late Latin decadence. The embroidery of purple and gold to which Conrad makes reference in the above passage could be taken to be his ultimate artistic attitude toward the political and Naturalistic *clichés* he observes. Although he denies such artistry in the realism of the world view he demonstrates ('It knits us in and it knits us out. It has knitted time, space, pain, death, corruption, despair and all the illusions, and nothing matters'[13]), he offers it as the only possible alternative in terms of a Decadent *écriture*.

It is this embroidery which appears symbolized in the 'lie' at the end of the novella, as Conrad underscores the process of dissimulation which is adopted by his narrator, Marlow. The lethal centre is 'pagitered' (to use the highly connotative term of Virginia Woolf) in the narrative which Marlow eventually offers to the Intended. Of the novelists discussed here, Conrad therefore is the most plastic in exposing the process whereby the narrative position has evolved through the distinct presentation of a fictional narrator. Whereas previous symbolism has been identified in the gap, the hyperbole, the prolongation in time, here it is demonstrated in the hollowing out of space: the decentring.

In view of such spatial mutation, the novella appropriately avoids sharply delineated characters and denotation in a thorough adoption of symbolic rhetoric. Kurtz remains a voice and a wraith, a vehicle for expression, crudely eviscerated, an emasculated frame from which hollow substance is extracted. Appropriately, Kurtz's expression is abbreviated, but the 'horror' is connotative and eloquent in its curtness. The Intended or abstract beauty remains gestures, hands illuminated with torches, the civilized or artistic spirit ironically nourished by delusion. Even the role of Marlow as a narrator removes him from character development as he remains ironically on the outside of things, circumventing the centre.

The novella acquires the quality of a modern myth and Goethean symbol. It has a mythopoeic dimension, with the tenor[14] of the Kurtz figure, the vehicle of Marlow who conveys that tenor, and the Muse which is the Intended all emerging from a metaphysical journey comparable with a Ulysses experience. Whereas Dostoevsky had focused on an archetype emerging out of a religious figure in his expression of Decadence, and James had constructed a fable for it, Conrad, in most modern terms, created a cultural myth.

And so *Heart of Darkness* comes full circle, as Marlow returns to the sepulchral citadel of 'civilization' and endorses the lie as the best of alternatives. The linear progression initiated at the beginning of the novel seems to have been annihilated as the circular form of movement is adopted in the novel. This is reminiscent of the patterns of return and recurrence in *Germinal* and *Jude the Obscure*.

Conrad's *oeuvre* is coloured by paradox. His major characters within his early period form a crew of waning figures, of outcasts, waifs, journeymen, lethal men, corpses and gibbets. Multiple lethal images pervade Conrad's major landscapes along with containers, shrouds, compartments, cabins harbouring souls like shells containing empty centres. These figures accumulate into a company of decadent modern Western men. As in the case of the other authors here examined, the characters are failures. Crises of identity occur in the moral isolation of these figures. The colonial experience serves to vilify the force of individual wills, reducing them to waifs in lost regions. And the savage landscapes of land or sea seem to threaten the validity of an already vulnerable ethical code. This is evident in works such as 'An Outpost of Progress' where two hardened Western men lose that sense of human community and become enemies, as one proceeds to destroy the other, shooting him unarmed within the setting of the African wilderness.

In the attempts which have been made to define Conrad's political imagination, there has been reference to frequent variation in the *degree* of his objection to the imperialist attitude in the course of his works.[15] From the moral point of view, however, the attitude is clearly one of censure, for in probing a political system from its moral foundation, Conrad went one step beyond the cultural and sociological concerns of the other Western authors here considered to observe the political implications of an anemic morality.

As Conrad approaches the topic of imperialism more forcefully from the moral than the political perspective, he is one of the first to question the 'imperialist' justification by the doctrine of civilization. As one of the 'creations' of Western civilization, Conrad viewed the manifestations of imperialism as symptomatic of the more individual social and moral decadence within. Of immediate and flagrant notice was of course the Boer War, which produced an atmosphere conducive to the writing of a problematic book such as *Heart of Darkness*. A moral conflagration occurred in him as well as in other notable writers to follow. Conrad, for instance, pre-dates in his fictional writing some of the attitudes caught by the British political economist J. A. Hobson, who in 1902 contributed to the emerging critical literature on imperialism in his book of that title. It is interesting that Hobson designated a degenerative tendency, not within imperialism *per se*, but in the shift from colonialism to the 'new' imperialism which he viewed as 'a retrograde step fraught with grave perils to the cause of civilization'.[16] In so doing, Hobson contributed to the derogatory connotation of the word 'imperialism' making it suspect as a watchword or 'masked one'. Conrad finds the fact of imperialism incongruous with the Naturalist, biological argument of progress.

In the literary context of Conrad's works, colonialism seems to be identified with Romanticism and a corresponding rhetoric which has lost its significance and sincerity of purpose. Decadence is envisaged as the outcome of that failing Romanticism that produced towering individuals such as Almayer, Wait and Kurtz, who crumble to death like modern-day versions of Ozymandias, a figure also eminently associated with the fall of empire.

Egotistical imaginations which represent excessive individualism cause their failures. Kurtz's megolomania especially demonstrates this as he utters without restraint: 'My Intended, my station, my career, my ideas' (147). Such figures paradoxically undermine their society as they loom above it, isolated in their individual identities which cause their demise in Romantic postures. As with Dostoevsky, an alternative of collectivity will be envisaged in his later writings, which are cast in a twentieth-century framework. Whereas in the case of the Russian novelist, it was seen in terms of an orthodox religious attitude, here in Conrad it is the political sphere – 'a move from private intentions to public systems'[17] as the critic Jacques Berthoud has stated. In Conrad, it also lies within the perspective of internationalism, specifically Pan-Europeanism, which the cosmopolitan writer viewed as a potentiality of collective Western fortitude. What Conrad demonstrates most convincingly in personal as well as national contexts is that individual weaknesses are accentuated once bonds with society are severed in a universe which has severed its bonds with man.

The background of imperialism is clearly a gauge for Conrad's understanding of decadence. What annihilates the normal destiny of such a man as Kurtz is the waning stage in which he is to perform his acts of vigour in a system which in the eyes of the author has lost its validity because of the falsification of motives. The paradoxical situation is that within the 'decaying' structure, such 'heroic' acts as Kurtz performs are turned into weakness. For, presumably, Kurtz has his strength: heading a gigantic enterprise, having power over his fellow men, controlling his destiny and that of his subordinates. Yet it is seen that every one of these attributes is cancelled out by forces beyond superficial visibility. Here is a character who in terms of a conventional code of the hero should be a positive force. But cast in an atmosphere of the deterioration of that code, his strength turns into weakness. Hence, the qualities can be viewed by the reader ironically and the code itself as losing its credibility because of the relaxation of its moral structures.

In fine, Conrad shares the concern over moral man in a critical condition in the throes of a crisis in values. It is as if the waning of the specifically religious figure, the Idiot, thirty years before (1869) had continued through the emaciation of the cultural figure, Jude, to its effacement in the hollow core that expresses the colossal Kurtz's Decadence. Of the writers considered here, Conrad is the most spectacular in his expression of decay. He conveys a mood of collective aging and cultural senescence. He sounds a toppling and resounding void. He emits a twilight and a dimming. The emasculation of Western man as he vividly presents it, the Faustian descendant of the Western Gothic mould, is most shocking as Conrad prepares the way for modern narrative in horrifically enacting the decentring.

7 The Decadent Style

The kind of Decadence noted in this study did not imply, in the period circumscribed, a corresponding decline in literary quality. It would certainly be a mistake in this case to associate the decline in values with a decadence in literary creativity, for the contrary occurred. The representative and renowned novels which emerged from this wavering Western society are monuments, constructed by a narrative art which is strong and powerful in depicting 'decline'.

The metaphysical unrest of these novelists produced an *écriture* – that is, a set of identifiable conventions encoded in the prose which can be exposed through an intertextual study of them. The novels, when juxtaposed, illuminate each other and demonstrate to what extent the mood and sense of urgency were contagious among these writers and germane to their time. Unconsciously these writers were together creating a Decadent style which transcended whatever literary intentions they might have individually proclaimed. For they did not simply follow the overt goals of Naturalism that, for example, a Zola or a Hardy had prescribed. A mimesis of a higher degree than mere representation of reality obtained; it captured through formal properties of style and structure an intangible spirit of the times. The intended referentiality became a basis for a leap to symbolization.

What is most interesting to observe is that Decadence is a dynamic narrative recording *process* of change rather than a static designation of a state. Whether it be, for example, a question of chronic crisis, postponement or decentring, it does not simply assert those patterns but demonstrates the process whereby they become indeed recognizable as a basis for subsequent conventionalization. It is as if these writers were drawing the readers into their intimacy of experiencing the breakdown as it occurs, to share with them an eschatological immediacy.

116

Dostoevsky's is the most obvious case. The aesthetic challenge that the composition of *The Idiot* afforded was more than just the creative pangs of an individual artist. It reflected the recognition of the obsolescence of a given type within the given society. And, as such, the work is not simply 'incomplete' as Dostoevsky might have thought it to be. For in actually attempting to depict 'the beautiful', his prose demonstrated the insufficiency of that topos. What might appear defective in terms of literary cohesiveness, of plot structure, character and composition, is only the creative process laid bare which confirms the loss of metaphysical substance. To be truly Decadent is to contain and divulge the process of such breakdown and deconstruction.

In fact, in many of the critical statements (found in notebook entries, letters and drafts) the writers admitted to the difficulties they were having both with their characters and with form. Like Dostoevsky, James and Hardy were troubled by the complexity of the types they were drawing (Isabel Archer and Sue Bridehead). In particular, James was conscious of 'the perhaps too great diffuseness of the earlier portion' of *The Portrait of a Lady*. Both he and Conrad specifically groped with their endings (as attested to in the notebook entry to *The Portrait of a Lady* and in the discussions between Ford Madox Ford and Conrad over *Heart of Darkness*). What is interesting is that in these admissions the writers are not fully aware that the difficulties were results, not causes, of the problematic context of their heroes and narrative structures.

The philosopher William Barrett has made a pertinent alliance of words in his article in defence of 'Existentialism as a Symptom of Man's Contemporary Crisis'.[1] There, he relates the word 'symptom' specifically to the word 'sign'. Just so, Decadent prose can also be said to enact a symptomatic code of waning signifiers. For throughout the novels there is a prevailing sense of a Western condition. So, in scrutinizing the signs of this narrative system, one can most consistently look for telling symptoms.

Among those symptomatic signs which are the most glaring in this grouping of novels are: the gap in Dostoevsky, the digression in James, the swelling in Zola, the constriction in Hardy, the hollow vacuity of Conrad. These are spatial features which seem to prefigure Modernist multidimensional morphology in contrast with classical Aristotelian linear constructs of narrative which proceed along temporal, chronological lines. It becomes evident that the narrative here is being challenged by new structuring devices which deconstruct previous ones and in so doing forcefully convey a sense of dislodgement and discomfiture. Above all a sense of unavoidable entrapment is communicated through these signs that seem persistently to provide a hiatus which is debilitating in terms of action and fulfilment of individual purpose. Insofar as these works are chief ones and representative of their times, they are innovative in terms of the breakdown they enact. Their stylistic dimension, structural rather than ornamental, puts them in a class of models.

It is necessary to bear in mind, as the critic György Vajda among others, has perceptively stated, that works rather than authors, belong to stylistic movements: 'Rarely can the entire lifework of a writer or an artist be considered as belonging to a given movement. Works rather than personalities, writers, painters, sculptors, or poets belong to movements.'[2] An author or artist may belong to several schools simultaneously spanning many styles in a long and prolific artistic career. This is true of the authors here designated, particularly of the later Dostoevsky or Conrad. Hence, if more modern novelists are gauged against the models here designated, it would be one particular facet of their work which would be identified with the Decadent style. Furthermore, the original novelists provide the basis for the conventions of a Decadent prose style. It is not surprising, for example, that disease should subsequently become one of the most commonly adopted metaphors.

The most substantial structural effect of Decadence is that upon the plot. In Dostoevsky, Zola and Hardy there is a salient diffusiveness. This has been identified in *The Idiot* with its episodes surfacing and disappearing throughout the novel. In Zola, too, there is a constant movement from one social sector to another, paralleling effects. In Hardy, there is a restless shifting from one configuration of human relationships to another, diffusing intensity. Such tendencies within the act of narrating have been termed by some as intradiagetic digressions, which are viewed as blurring the plot sequence. In James, the entire work is ultimately conceived as a digression.

This merits closer examination. *The Idiot*, for example, is constructed through a series of episodes which make the principal character avoid any single motive. Myshkin's attraction for Nastasya is blurred by the advances of Aglaya. The factors of his inheritance and his mission wane in submissiveness to intervening events: the nihilistic assault and the party. His relationship with Rogozhin lacks any emotive consistency because of that character's vagrant entrances and exits. Most significant, a proliferation of polyphonic voices from minor characters such as Ippolit, Lebedev and Radomsky occurs sporadically throughout the novel, gaining ascendancy over action.

The same apparent laxness of construction is true of *Germinal* and *Nana*. It is as if *Germinal* consisted of a series of rehearsals for the uprising that Etienne desires to effectuate. Conceived intermittently, Etienne's relationship with Catherine is never firm; the intrigues of Madame Hennebeau, Jeanlin and Souvarine are interludes which deter the reader's focal attention, so that Rasseneur's strike seems more important than Etienne's. The only decisive action of *Nana* is the eventual death of the character by smallpox at the end of the novel: throughout her relationship with the Count in the course of the novel, Nana remains completely static as an emblem. In fact, it is noted that Zola relegated his plot to a subsidiary position. He admitted in his draft to the novel: 'In my work, the dramatic action is completely secondary' (*Chez moi le drame est tout à fait secondaire*) (1666). His drafts are testimony to the fact that his novels proceed by association of ideas and multiplication of scenic effects rather than by actual causal connections. *L'Assommoir* and *L'Argent* also show tendencies towards dilution, given two very dilutable elements: wine and money.

Hardy's novels abound in readily apparent setbacks and persistent detours, often interestingly expressed in geographic terms. The plot's progress is halted periodically by predicaments which make for new starts. In *Jude*, the first eighty-nine pages of the Wessex edition (or first part) seem to be a detour from the intended route as Arabella functions as a major obstacle or interruption to Jude's progress: 'He had at last found himself clear of Marygreen and Alfredston: he was out of his apprenticeship, and with his tools at his back seemed to be in the way of making a *new start*' (89). Characters are readily *led astray* by impulse or dream. A loss of direction is frequently communicated. Emphasis throughout Hardy's novels is on the static quality of relationships which lead nowhere because of snags and gaps between characters. Hardy introduces the Decadent situation which becomes an objective correlative of this stagnant condition. In *Tess of the d'Urbervilles*, for example, two relationships coexist, as the principal character fluctuates nervously between her alliances with Alex and with Claire, and *regresses* to her first relationship at the end, unfulfilled. The same instability abounds in *The Return of the Native*, where the couples constantly interchange. This becomes fully typical in *Jude the Obscure*, where Sue vacillates between her alliances with Jude and with Phillotson, and Jude is in a stalemate between Sue and Arabella. The scene toward the end in the Temperance Hotel demonstrates the ready substitution of one woman for another. In all instances, there is no progress beyond the recognition of these relationships and the recurring problematics which surface at junctures throughout the novels. Furthermore, a statement like 'he was mentally approaching the position which Sue had occupied when he first met her' (373) ironically demonstrates to what extent the itinerary, if it be considered one at all, is a mental one.

An obsessive circularity replaces linear direction and determination in these novels. Intentionality is obviated in most cases: the Idiot's mission and that of Lambert Strether's, though hardly comparable in substance, are never achieved. The goals of Etienne Lantier and Jude, political and personal, are not reached. It is even interesting that if most of these novels involve an itinerary of some kind (Strether's to Paris, Jude's to Christminster, Myshkin's to St Petersburg, Etienne's to Lyon, even Marlow's to the Congo) no progress is achieved as the characters return to their original conditions, and their goals are characteristically thwarted. (Perhaps they should be better termed as 'excursions'.)

In the case of James, Hardy and Conrad, the specific process of *avoidance* of plot and its classical resolution (ending) has been recognized. It is to be remembered that *The Ambassadors* particularly annihilated the plot, through the one big digression, Maria Gostrey: 'Strether filled up the time, as he had so often filled it before, by going to see Miss Gostrey' (291). Strether, whose only moves are mental ones, delays effective narrative action (failing in his mission). Even the more simplistic novel, *The American*, leaves an inconclusiveness to its ending (averting the anticipatory comic structure) as the family renegues on its decision of marriage, and the previously confident Newman is left in a quandary. *The Portrait of a Lady* provides an entirely new alternative of ending just at the point when a belaboured reconcilement and settling are anticipated. As for Hardy, his sense of recurring crisis leaves the reader *in medias res*, for the problems he perceives remain issues which are consistently harassing, compounding complications instead of leading to resolutions. The only finality which he offers is death, which appears in these cases as artificial conclusions and not intrinsic elements of the plot structure. Coming to Conrad, his *Heart of Darkness* distinctly avoids the meeting with the centre, as most of the narrative is preparation and withdrawal, the climax is *anticlimactic* and the resolution tentative. The various episodes which lead to Kurtz only delay and digress from the point in question. In the stories, as well, marginality is displacing centrality.

Of the novels discussed in this study, it has been seen how *The Ambassadors* and *Heart of Darkness* (on the very margins of the century) are most viscerally concerned with the extrication of plot. Although all the novels are mythopoeic to some degree, these two mentioned seem fully reflexive in their demonstration of plot deconstruction. Both writers have a highly material contact with the 'figure' of plot. Kurtz can be considered the plot's corpse, which is discovered through the *récit* of Marlow. Strether's narrative perspective of postponement dissipates an aborted plot (foetus). Both works are technical insofar as the fate of the plot is their central issue.

It is noticeable, too, that rampant eschatological syndromes and image patterns intrude in these novels, functioning on mythical and actual levels to prolong the process of ending. Imminence is made *immanent*, as a synchronic presence rather than a diachronic one. A sense of ending transpires from the onset of the novels – joining the alpha and the omega. Dostoevsky's *Idiot* is actually foreshadowed by authentic eschatological symbols of the apocalypse: the reference to Holbein's picture as AntiChrist, Lebedev's interpretation of the Apocalypse (with the third horse), Ippolit's confession and scorpion dream (the beast reference). The relationship of Nastasya and Rogozhin is provocative of the paradigm of Apocalyptic whore and the beast – which becomes haunting in Zola's *Nana* (the rapport of Nana and Count Muffat). In *Germinal*, the mine itself simulates the beast (acquiring animalistic characteristics of churning) and is the source of a kind of Apocalyptic conflagration, as is the jungle (also associated with bestial imagery or railways) in *Heart of Darkness*. In Hardy's *Return of the Native*, the heath is described as an eschatological terrain, containing both the beginning and the ending and 'awaiting the final overthrow' (at the beginning of the novel). In James's works, reference to ending and darkening heightens the sense of moral ambiguity: Strether associates his postponement with 'extinction', Isabel's world darkens in an Apocalyptic way as she perceives her failure to achieve integrity. Darkness prevails as the dominant tone in most of these novels: perplexities are prolonged as immense obscurities (ink-like blackness) overwhelm, for example, *Germinal*, *Jude the Obscure* and *Heart of Darkness*.

There are also certain mysterious and disturbing characters throughout this fiction which function as formal devices to incarnate the death factor obsessively in the narrative. These figures include the most obvious Wait in *The Nigger of the 'Narcissus'*, Fred Touchett in James's *Portrait of a Lady*, Ippolit in *The Idiot*, Bonnemort in *Germinal*, the reddleman in Hardy's *Return of the Native* and Father Time in *Jude the Obscure*. Their intermittent appearances occur in an almost technical manner to provide constant breakdown and rupture in the narrative; relationships may be broken in their presence as well. It has been seen how, for example, in Conrad's *The Nigger of the 'Narcissus'* the emblematic figure of Wait serves to break down the cohesiveness of the crew, providing the climate for a general moral weakening. His death is a determinant factor releasing the ending. Other obsessive dying specimens are Ippolit and Fred Touchett. Ippolit, a shadow to the Idiot, is an eschatological presence underlying the sequence of events, signifying and incarnating the process of ending, extenuating it. Significantly, it is he who utters the impossibility of expressing the essence of things or the idea; as a ghost-like figure he undermines ontological validity. In the case of *The Portrait of a Lady*, Fred Touchett, also dying of tuberculosis, represents a missed identity which Isabel fails to seize. It is interesting that Isabel waits throughout the novel for the dying process to terminate, for the waning substance to be transformed into a ghost. Ralph indicates the remnants of plot being eradicated, and through him Isabel confronts this process and the emergence of a symbol. In the case of Zola, Bonnemort, who appears as ancient, contains death in his very name, and haunts Germinal from the very beginning, as he is the first figure which Etienne meets, setting the eschatological tone and destiny from the start. He too prevails throughout the novel, despite his weakened condition in insufferable surroundings, to prefigure the outcome. The reddleman in *The Return of the Native* functions in a similar way, colouring the destiny of the characters from the beginning as his occupa-

tional identity is threatened with extinction. Both minor characters are environmental products: extensions of mine and heath.
Ultimately, Hardy's Father Time is the most spectacular
eschatological agent, forecasting beyond narrative time an inevitable Apocalypse. In the case of the particular novel, he determines in an almost mechanical way the course of the narrative,
ironically substituting for stalemate a negative action.

In all these instances, death is a constant factor affecting the
contours of narrative. Its pre-eminence is made thematic through
the technique of these human figures, visibly affecting structure.
These paradigms function as signals which prefigure the course of
the narrative and disrupt the normative flow of plot sequence.
They create blockage in the narrative and forecast the failure of
the major characters.

There is also the power of the image to suspend action in these
Decadent novels (as prefigured by Huysmans); such images
expand into scenes or static portraits which interrupt the flow of
narrative by halting visions. This is the case, for example, in the
contemplation of the bed in *Nana*, in the description of the Holbein
painting in *The Idiot*, in the observation of the Oxford buildings in
Jude the Obscure, in Marlow's view of Kurtz in *Heart of Darkness* and
in Isabel's meditative vigil over the dying fire in *The Portrait of a
Lady*. Such scenes endow the prose with a static character.

What has been termed by some as adjectival vagueness in
particular reference to Conrad is noticeable throughout this
Decadent narrative in the extended descriptions. The vague
adjectives and abstract nouns trigger affective images as in
Conrad's expression 'the horror', in Hardy's reference to the
'nebulosity of a scene', in the obscurity of the epithet of Jude, in
James's use of the word 'wonderful' to describe Madame de
Vionnet's affair, and in the reference to 'flabbiness' by Conrad,
Zola and Dostoevsky. On the syntactical level, active verbs give
way to intransitive ones. There are, for example, the static
declarations of Zola ('C'était . . .') and of James ('Then there we
were') – which unexpectedly produce dramatic effects. A distinct
nominal style emerges in much of the narrative.

To use the Nietzschean terms of *The Gay Science*, there is a
Dionysian process of constructive fragmentation, which destroys
the duality of the metaphor (tenor-vehicle), leading to the
independence of the vehicle. In other words, the literal quality of
the metaphors is exploited. David Lodge, in his book *The Language*

of Fiction,[3] has described a form of this process as 'heightened cliché' in the case of James, who puts Chad and Madame de Vionnet literally 'in the same boat'. Throughout this fiction, there is a marked 'literality'; that is, reality takes on and imitates the metaphoric analogies. To express indulgence, for example, Zola floods the streets of Paris with wine, and a willing suspension of disbelief is created in the reader's reception.

There is a marked tendency toward conceptualization in this Decadent *écriture*, often conveyed by a monadogic style, whereby writers isolate elementary components and invest them with concrete functions. The most obvious example is Zola's anthropomorphism (a countercurrent to 'dehumanization'). He singles out concepts such as flesh, money, capital, labour, alcohol and observes them as a mechanism affecting the individual and society. They appear as constants and acquire the standing of concrete realities contending as human agents. As abstract nouns they include a host of predicates and function as vehicles (replacing the active verbs). The use of synecdoche is particularly striking with respect to this technique: a principal part is often made to refer to the whole, and the transfer is immediate. Zola's statement 'an entire society turning upon a backside' (*toute une société se ruant sur le cul*) (*Nana*, 1665) is the most powerful example of this fusion of the literal and the figurative.

An abstraction (in the use of language) affects the level of characters, as names are personified. Examples are Father Time in *Jude the Obscure* (demonstrating the eschatological), Kurtz in *Heart of Darkness* (meaning 'brief', 'summing it up') and Wait in the *The Nigger of the 'Narcissus'* (creating suspension in the narrative), Isabel Archer in *The Portrait of a Lady* (suggesting the arch-like construction of her appearance), Myshkin in *The Idiot* (his 'mouse-like' implication), Bonnemort (death implied), Sue Bridehead of Hardy and Daisy Miller of James (both suggesting pure but waning flowers). Not only are their names abstractions, however, but also their personalities, as has been seen. A certain distance is maintained between the reader and characters such as Myshkin, Nana, Archer, Jude and Kurtz who, interestingly, share a common marked quality of abstractness and remoteness. (Some readers may even be offended by their coldness or impenetrability.) They remain evanescent, ambivalent, not readily seized: described appropriately in terms such as 'disembodied', 'bodiless', 'phantasmal', 'inconsistent', 'amorphous', 'anomaly'. Their relevance is more paradigmatic than psychological; their presence more morphological than distinctly tangible.

A ponderous quality characterizes this prose as it reverberates in multilayers and often baffles the reader with a sense of puzzlement. In Conrad, there is the weightiness of individual words and expressions such as the irony of the hearsay, 'He [Kurtz] is a remarkable man', or the haunting understatement of the utterance, 'the horror'. The surplus effect and duplication throughout Zola's prose overwhelms and saturates the readers. In James there are the innuendoes and repercussions of individual statements which expand and harass compulsively. In Dostoevsky, there are the multiple voices of commentary within the narrative (Lebedev – Ippolit – Rogozhin) and in Hardy, the generalized, philosophic conclusions ('colossal inconsistencies', 'moral hobgoblins') of the authorial commentator.

In all these writers there is a claustrophobic, stultifying atmosphere of extended rumination, dramatized most disturbingly by the all-too-reflective child of *Jude the Obscure*. Two Western archetypes of contemplative man which dwell within these works contribute to this climate: the Hamlet syndrome and the Faustian imperative. The works are informed by the Hamlet theme of morbid self-consciousness reflected in the extenuated analysis which produces doubt in the characters and creates conflicts between thought and action. This is true particularly of the Jude effect: coloured by a dark sensitivity which makes him falter and intensifies his inner turmoil, he is caught in a Hamlet-like trance of inaction. Given to the habit of 'ratiocinative meditativeness' (to use Coleridge's term for the Hamlet condition) the dark character seems fraught with paralysis. Many of Conrad's characters are debilitated, as has been seen, by the paralysis of the will, and James's characters persistently stall in meditative doubt, as is the case of Strether. Even the Idiot can be viewed as being immobilized by a kind of philosophic perplexity. In addition, the Faustian archetype is intimated in these works, especially in Conrad and Hardy. It is particularly relevant to Conrad's colossal figure in *Heart of Darkness* and there are ironic innuendoes of it in *Jude the Obscure*: the futile intellectual atmosphere of Faust's study scene is mimicked by the modern scepticism of Jude's act of burying his books.

More generally speaking, atmospheric effects are created by the sultry prose of Hardy, for example, and the inebriated one of Zola, as a sort of physicality (beyond mere sensuality) is ascribed to the lexicon, contagiously. A distinct aura of contamination affects the works as the prose gets infected by an iterative tendency toward negation. The germs of the Decadent narrative (whether they be postponement, hyperbole, etc.) grow persistently in the recurring situations which become identifiable patterns in each text. Disconnected synonyms and repetitions such as the myriad 'deteriorating words' in Zola and the choral refrains of Conrad and Hardy contribute to the sense of fragmentation.

The language itself, in addition to the structure and the paradigms, is affective and connotative. In the most dynamic instances of Zola, it is as if words flow like wine out from the source on to the pavements inundating the page. In James, where the words are restrained, the inarticulate becomes a presence unto itself, deeply communicated but not expressed. A semblance of superficiality paradoxically translates the essential, creating the effect of a false scent. Throughout this narrative, words grow and diminish from understatement to hyperbole. This elasticity of language ascribes a poetic quality to this form of fiction, as the words themselves are not only descriptive but an expanding reality that the characters and the reader or interpreter have to contend with.

It has been noticed how these novels proceed from archetype to myth. *Nana*, for example, transcends the Naturalistic portraits of its contemporaries such as Huysmans's *Marthe* or Edmond de Goncourt's *La Fille Elisa*, for it is not simply the specific description of a single prostitute but of a power and proportion greater than an individual one. In fact, the character Nana herself seems to be specifically speaking on her author's behalf when, commenting on a so-called contemporary novel she is reading, she denigrates the genre for its claims to authenticity. When Nana is described as a 'devourer of men' (*mangeuse d'hommes*), one realizes her symbolic function: she is both archetypal as a prostitute and mythically representative of her society. Some of Hardy's characters are mythic in a primordial way, relating to Biblical or Greek specimens, Adams, Eves or Proserpines; the existential element in these characters creates a myth of modernism. When Sue Bridehead of *Jude the Obscure* is described as a 'colossal inconsistency', her larger significance is also emphasized. Isabel Archer, with her symbolic name, seems greater than life in her androgynous dimensions. This leads to the figure of

Kurtz, who is over seven feet tall and whose character is viewed as mythic according to the previously quoted: 'All Europe contributed to the making of Kurtz'. Although individual qualities are assigned to these personages, they are magnified for scrutiny and become representative of phenomena within the corpus of society. The Naturalistic method is directed toward the general rather than the particular.

That such tendency toward mythification has been achieved in this period can be demonstrated by reference to later works, such as Thomas Mann's which treats Decadent personalities in a mythic perspective. By the time of *Death in Venice* in 1911, a historical distance from the Decadent stylistics is communicated through the twentieth-century ironic tone with which Mann treats the subject of Decadence. The work is not involved in the creation of the myth but in an observation of it. Hence the stereotype of the Decadent, whose characteristics are recognized, not revealed. The work is comprehensive in combining the aesthetic and the psychological aspect of the Decadent hero. For as well as being the artist expiring in the contemplation of classic beauty, Gustave Aschenbach, just past his fiftieth birthday, is a kind of Jamesian character, dissatisfied with his non-participation in life while ironically being an observer of it as an eminent biographer. The literal creation of a Decadent climate proceeds along lines which can be discerned as conventional: the sirocco disease, the Latin analogy, the images of Apocalytic beasts, the Byzantine edifices, the eschatological reveries contained in the Dionysian visions. Of foremost significance in this work is not the identification of these elements, but the narrative tone with which the author treats what has become a readily recognizable myth.

In returning to Decadent prose, one finds that its most consistent narrative voice is that of a diagnostician. This should hardly be surprising given the fact that much of the influence on Naturalistic prose was experimental medicine and the scientific values of the times with the writer emulating the physician as observer and documenter. In *Heart of Darkness* it is as if the discourse of Marlow is being given as *evidence* from which to draw conclusions, as the author-narrator receives the testimony of the persona-narrator. In Hardy's prose, the narrator is intent as observer and recorder (even historian) of certain apparent symptoms of mood and condition, and it is significant that a doctor even surfaces in *Jude the Obscure* to comment on Father Time. In James, the heroes are treated as specimens, cases in point, with the 'our hero' to remind the reader that it is a case-history. In Zola, the narrator *scans* certain situations and processes an array of samplings. In Dostoevsky, the narrator interestingly seems to be proving the diagnosis made from the start. These narrators seem to be accumulating evidence without prognosis as they remain distanced from the conditions they uncover, although concerned about them.

Specific descriptions of new, emerging states are encapsulated in diagnostic expressions such as 'prostration', 'posture of prolonged impermanence' (James), 'modern man in a quandary', 'phlegmatic passivity' and 'the ache of modernism' (Hardy), 'wayside quagmire' (Conrad). These can be in the form of entire statements, as the one referring to the apoplexy of inordinate capital trading in Zola ('une pléthore d'affaires véreuses gonflait le marché, le congestionnait jusqu'à l'apoplexie' – *L'Argent*, 260) or to an actual condition, such as the epilepsy of *The Idiot*. Such description is heightened by a technical vocabulary with words such as those found in Hardy's *Jude the Obscure*: 'epicene' (reference to Sue Bridehead), 'conundrum' (reference to her puzzling conduct), 'volatile essence' (reference to the nature of love).

In the diagnosis of such states, the author seems to demonstrate *how* such states occur – and their inevitability as outcomes of specific combinations of circumstances and environment. In this respect, the narrative adheres closely to the premises established by Zola in his widely-read and representative document of the time (1880) *Le Roman expérimental*, which merits reconsideration in this context. Despite the fact that Zola was a greater poet than he ever claimed to be (with a tendency toward illumination in his writing comparable to Rimbaud's at times) and that he did *not* follow the prosaic, utilitarian aims of his theory of fiction, there are certain elements which he singles out in this document that are involved in Decadent prose. It is to be remembered that Zola insisted on the 'comment' (how) of phenomena rather than the 'pourquoi' (why). In observing the interactions of the individual and society, Zola was concerned with the dynamics of those relations. His eye probed the mechanism of behaviour and he objected to being called fatalistic since the determinism he uncovered was based on certain controls or factors which could be altered. Much of Decadent fiction actually explores and records the malfunctioning produced by certain combinations of heredity, environment and historical epoch, as has been seen.

Furthermore, Zola's emphasis was upon *method* (combining experience and observation) which he distinguished from style, viewed as a superficial trait. If anything was to mark the writers of his time, he stated, it would be the *treatment* of the subject matter: 'Basically, I consider that method becomes form itself' (Au fond, j'estime que la méthode atteint la forme elle-même) (*Le Roman expérimental*[4]). Zola's document provides further justification for grouping these novelists together in a common methodology which could be called symptomology. In considering the word style in its greater meaning of structure, form and method, it saves its lesser meaning for the conventions which would follow in the enactment of the method.

In retrospect, when James was talking about the 'figure in the carpet', in his story of that title (1896), it can be said that he was tantalizing and challenging the reader to discover his Decadent style, to be distinguished from Realism. The story itself is cast in James's characteristic terms of the missed experience as the narrator-critic is unable to detect the aesthetic principle underlying a certain artist's (named Hugh Vereker) fiction. Interestingly, James describes this quest for a narrative string in Aesthetic terms even though it is not a question of Aestheticism *per se*: it is subtle, not intended for the vulgar, it is infatuating, and those who have the 'secret' behold it and die: it is antithetical to life. He puts the reader in a superior position to his narrator, beckoning him to become sensitive and receptive to the code.

In James's 'The Art of Fiction' (1884), in Hardy's 'The Science of Fiction' (1891) and in Conrad's *Prefaces*, there are hints by the writers that their art is conceived as symbolic mimesis distinct from realistic copyism. Without any overt formulation of specifically symbolist prose, these writers in their literary prefaces reject the realistic and naturalistic tendencies of their time and hint at an aesthetic of 'the part'. It is interesting that they each regard their narrative function as a Daedalian one, as they proceed from the rudiments of 'the piece' (James), 'the half and quarter views' (Hardy), 'the rescued fragment' (Conrad) to evoke the larger pattern.

As far as the relationship of Decadence to Romanticism is concerned, there have been of course many theories connecting the two, as in the case of Mario Praz, who views it as an extension, even in its rebellious position against the former movement. The flower image is the most dramatic focus for a consideration of its links with a mother movement because nature was the matrix of that former movement. As has been noticed, the artificial flower of the orchid in Aestheticism replaces the roses and daffodils of Romanticism. But in the context of Decadence as here proposed, nature is simply heightened, not improved upon, as in the examples of the heath or of the jungle. Romanticism as a referential system for Decadence is particularly striking in Conrad's works, which often minimize the Romantic element by allocating it to the substructure of the *récit*. As observed in this study, Decadence is indeed nurtured in Romanticism, for without the moral background, there would not have been the moral traumas which create the Decadent style.

Decadence can best be envisaged in a pivotal position with respect to Modernism. It can be seen as a preparation for the *avant-garde*, as it begins the process of breakdown of certain traditional facets of classical narrative such as plot, integrated character and verisimilitude of setting. Whereas ellipses, analepses and prolepses are (used in an affirmative way) structural elements in modern fiction, as Gerard Genette has aptly illustrated in his study of Proust,[5] here in this Decadent prose, the gaps function in an opposite manner: disintegrating character and diffusing plot. One is well aware that in the case of Proust, for example, a seemingly marginal detail may gain full significance in retrospect, budding into significance at a later point in the novel, when it achieves fruition. Digressiveness and marginality are rendered significant in a synchronic construct. Here the contrary is true, and false scents are diffused as potential details are never actualized or rendered effective, creating negative effects of abortive births and, at times, regression instead of maturation and ripening at subsequent phases. James's is the most vivid case of the failure of completion as an aesthetic: of the haunting and debilitating presence of the absent which becomes the unfulfilled, containing that which will never be expressed in the 'secret' of narrative (to use Tzvetan Todorov's term[6]), and eliminating the ontological by denying it narrative space. This emptiness is not yet the fertile terrain to be filled by the moderns with new signals but, instead, vacancies, frustrating communication among the characters, made manifest by the telling symptoms of narrative displacement. On the artistic level, Conrad emotionally transmits the horror of displacement as he exposes a fictional narrator to it.

Inconsistencies are produced by these spatial and temporal gaps within and between characters and situations in Decadent prose. In Modernist fiction, where such lapses are frequent and assumed as normal, such discontinuity often termed as anachrony identifies creative intervals, providing for a constructive process of convergence. In this Decadent prose, they instead foster divergences. This study has identified the range of those tropes from the constricted negative spaces of Hardy, the intraspaces of Dostoevsky, the interspatial gaps of James, to the ultra-ballooning of Zola and the hollow voiding of Conrad. In the particular juxtaposition of Dostoevsky and James, one can best observe the process of symbol-making: for James goes beyond Dostoevsky (and his symbolic implications) by actually filling the gap (which was the space for Dostoevsky's 'missed idea' that can never be expressed) by a ghost, or symbol.

In this respect, Lukács's concept of symbolic modernism (which he applies to Flaubert, Zola and Joyce) does have some validity in categorizing this prose. It is ironic that Lukács himself used the term pejoratively to designate a prose which departed from historical realism and classical forms of narrative. The elements that he singled out as destroying the historical novel, such as excessive description, disproportionate observation, suspension of action, are precisely those which nurture modernist developments in the novel. And one can say that in its very divergence from classical models of the novel, there is even the creation of a transitional model.

The novelists here dealt with contribute to a development of symbolism in prose. In expressing the common denominator of excess which they locate in their period, it is not surprising that their style should range from overstatement to understatement. For in their attempts to identify a condition of disequilibrium in their society, their narrative features the margins of deterrence from and aberration of the previous norm. The word Decadence has here been taken to refer to a loosening of literary structures, defining a gap or rupture, tracing through various defaults the slippage from a holistic universe to a fragmented one, from well-defined relationships to undirected ones.

At the same time, these authors distance themselves from the characters they are portraying. They do not themselves succumb to the disparity between the code of ethics they have struggled with in their own lives and the undermining of it which is occurring around them. They are instead observers of the phenomenon of the rites of passage. They demonstrate the qualities here delineated, such as 'postponement', 'perplexity', 'sense of crisis', 'consumption', as if they wanted to seize what is fast slipping.

Postponement becomes a holding off of the sensed Apocalypse – let us struggle a little longer with what we have held dear before we plunge into the void and have to take a new action along with new attitudes, they seem to say. Even criticism in terms of old establishments such as imperialism is self-referential (that is, within the caste system in which it has thrived and not from the frontiers of a new system). They fear Darwinism without having coped with it. They fear the new use of language and do not engage in its polysemantic character. The group designated here as Decadent is decadent because it deviates from the standard use of language but within the context of that language; this group does not create or try to create a new semantics because it is too conscious of the *glissement* of the old and not quite ready to do away with it. This group of authors saw what was happening and recorded it in various fashions as has been observed in this study, without becoming part of the disengagement and destruction.

In fine, Decadence as has been used here is a relative value applicable to those who still cling to an *absolute* system; without this transitional era of Decadence there could have been no modernism. The magical alembic is the abiding symbol of the distillation of that Decadence into art.

Notes and References

Chapter 1: The Grammar of Decadence: Perversity, Paradox and Perplexity

1. See Michel Foucault, *Les Mots et les choses* (Paris: Gallimard, 1966) pp. 396–7. This and all other translations from the French quoted in this book are mine.
2. See Preface to *The Case of Wagner* (1888), where Nietzsche distinguished himself from Wagner, stating: 'I am just as much a child of my age as Wagner – i.e., I am a decadent. The only difference is that I recognized the fact, that I struggled against it. . . . My greatest preoccupation hitherto has been the problem of "decadence" ' – *The Complete Works of Friedrich Nietzsche*, vol. 8, ed. Oscar Levy (New York: Russell and Russell, 1964) pp. xxix–xxx.
3. Friedrich Nietzsche, *The Portable Nietzsche*, ed. Walter Kaufmann (New York: Viking Press, 1968) p. 208. The translations of Nietzsche quoted in the text are Kaufmann's.
4. Ibid., p. 208. Actually *Muschel* can mean mussel and Nietzsche might have had that image in mind for a symbol of a living entity rather than the notion of an inert shell.
5. Ibid., p. 208.
6. Ibid., p. 209.
7. Ibid., p. 483.
8. See Roger Bauer's article tracing this, 'Décadence: histoire d'un mot et d'une idée', in *Cahiers roumains d'études littéraires* (Bucharest, 1978) pp. 55–78.
9. From Preface by Théophile Gautier to Charles Baudelaire, *Les Fleurs du mal* (Paris: Lemerre, 1868) p. 20.
10. See J. K. Huysmans, 'Préface écrite vingt ans après le roman', in *A Rebours*, ed. Marc Fumaroli (Paris: Gallimard, 1977).
11. Huysmans, *A Rebours*, p. 190.
12. Ibid., p. 191.
13. See Stéphane Mallarmé's poem, 'Prose pour Des Esseintes' (1884). According to the notes of the Pléiade edition of Mallarmé's works (Paris: Gallimard, 1945), this poem was written in response to a letter of 1882 from Huysmans indicating the plan of *A Rebours* and asking Mallarmé to send him some poems.
14. Huysmans, *A Rebours*, p. 332.
15. Arthur Symons, *A Study of Oscar Wilde* (London: Charles J. Sawyer, Grafton House, 1930) p. 24.
16. Christopher S. Nassaar, *Into the Demon Universe: A Literary Exploration of Oscar Wilde* (New Haven and London: Yale University Press, 1974) p. 66.

17. Oscar Wilde, 'The Decay of Lying', in *Complete Works* (London: Collins, 1948) p. 978.
18. Arthur Symons, 'The Decadent Movement in Literature', in *Dramatis Personae* (Freeport, NY: Books for Libraries Press, rpt 1971) pp. 96–7.
19. Ibid., p. 116.
20. Preface to first issue of *The Savoy* (January 1896) cited by Frances Winwar, *Oscar Wilde and the Yellow Nineties* (Garden City, NY: Blue Ribbon Books, 1941) p. 244: for a discussion of the yellow symbolism, see this book.
21. Guy Michaud in his *Message poétique du Symbolisme* (Paris: Librairie Nizet, 1947) identifies a Belgian group of young poets such as Rodenbach, Verhaeren, Samain, Laforgue, Moréas as Decadents. Michaud envisages Decadence as a lyrical stage in the *poetic* revolution that was Symbolism.
22. Paul Bourget, *Essais de psychologie contemporaine* (Paris: Lemerre, 1883) pp. 22–3.
23. Ibid., p. 14.
24. Ibid., p. 25.
25. Ibid., p. 25.
26. Max Nordau, *Degeneration*, trans. from the second edition of the German work by George L. Mosse (New York: Howard Fertig, 1968) p. 2.
27. Oswald Spengler's term in *The Decline of the West* (1918–22) to identify Western man in the post-Medieval period. See *The Decline of the West*, 2 vols (New York: Alfred Knopf, 1926–8); originally published as *Der Untergang des Abendlandes*, 2 vols (Munich: C. H. Beck'sche Verlagsbuchhandlung, 1918, 1922).
28. Critical literature on decadence has been profuse but the definition of the term among literary critics remains eclectic; so much so that Henri Peyre called for the dismissal of the term. There are those who envisage it as an ultimate phase of Romanticism, the leading proponent of which is Mario Praz (*The Romantic Agony*, 1933, rpt London: Fontana Library, 1960). Others, in sharp contrast, regard it in connection with Modernism: Matei Calineseu's is the most comprehensive survey as he views its interface with the *avant-garde* in his book entitled *Faces of Modernity* (Indiana University Press, 1977). Jean Pierrot, who emphasizes the Aestheticism of the decadent period delimited as 1880–1900 in his book *L'Imaginaire Décadent* (Paris: Presses Universitaires de France, 1972), views its intermediary status between Classicism and Modernism. Renato Poggioli, whose intention was to write a book on the subject under the Baudelairean title *The Autumn of Ideas*, distinguished decadence from the *avant-garde* by its firm identification with the past. In his dialectical view of the term, he associated it with Barbarism, which he regarded as the natural nemesis of a decadent civilization – see his article 'Qualis Artifex Pereo! or Barbarism and Decadence', in *Harvard Library Bulletin*, XIII, 1 (Winter 1959) pp. 135–49. Another cultural view of decadence is A. E. Carter's *The Idea of Decadence in French Literature: 1830–1900* (University of Toronto Press, 1958) which regards it as a serious preoccupation in the nineteenth century's spiritual assessment of Western civilization. Other critics see it in more parochial national contexts such as George Ross Ridge in *The Hero in French Decadent Literature* (University of Georgia Press, 1961) and William Eickhorst in *Decadence in German Fiction* (Denver: Swallow, 1953). In a recent challenge of

the word in *Decadence: The Strange Life of an Epithet* (New York: Farrar, Straus and Giroux, 1975), Richard Gilman brings out its variableness as well as its diachronic and cyclical prevalence throughout literature and therefore desists from identifying and pursuing any single facet of its meaning.

29. See Suzanne Nalbantian, *The Symbol of the Soul from Hölderlin to Yeats* (New York and London: Columbia University Press and Macmillan, 1977).

30. For a provocative discussion of a synchronic view of the apocalyptic paradigm, see Frank Kermode's *The Sense of an Ending* (Oxford University Press, 1966). His frame of reference is entirely different, as he identifies links between Ancient and Modernist 'absurd-oriented' literature (skirting the *fin-de-siècle* period) and regarding the apocalyptic paradigm as especially endemic to modern fiction.

Chapter 2: *Dostoevsky and the Gap of Insufficiency*

1. Letter to Sofia Alexandrovna, 1 January 1868, in *Letters of Fyodor Michailovitch Dostoevsky to his Family and Friends*, trans. Ethel Colburn Mayne (London: Chatto and Windus, 1914) p. 135.

2. Fyodor Dostoevsky, *The Idiot*, trans. David Magarshack (New York: Penguin Books, 1955) p. 146. All parenthetical page references in the text are to this translation.

3. See Chapter 1, p. 14 above.

4. *Letters*, trans. Mayne, p. 135.

5. See *The Idiot*, p. 563: 'modern man is more diffuse and, I assure you, it is this that prevents him from being such a complete human being as they were in those days.'

6. William Butler Yeats, 'The Autumn of the Body', in *Essays and Introductions* (New York: Collier, 1961) p. 191; first published as 'The Autumn of the Flesh', *The Dublin Daily Express*, 3 December 1898.

7. See Letter to Strachov, 18 May 1871, in *Letters*, trans. Mayne, p. 207.

8. Nietzsche, *The Portable Nietzsche*, ed. Kaufmann, p. 603.

9. Ibid., p. 633.

10. Ibid., p. 603.

Chapter 3: *Henry James and the Poetics of Postponement*

1. See Henry James, Preface to *The Portrait of a Lady*, New York edition, vol. 3 (New York: Charles Scribner's, 1908) pp. vi–vii. All parenthetical page references to James's novels and tales are from this edition.

2. Percy Lubbock, *The Craft of Fiction* (New York: Viking Press, rpt 1957) p. 167.

3. See 'Project of Novel by Henry James', in *The Notebooks of Henry James*, ed. F. O. Matthiessen (New York: Oxford University Press, 1947) p. 414.

4. See James's undated discussion (presumed to be late 1880 or early 1881) of *The Portrait of a Lady* in *Notebooks*, ed. Matthiessen, p. 15.

5. *Notebooks*, ed. Matthiessen, p. 18.

6. Ibid., p. 18.
7. Ibid., p. 18.
8. T. S. Eliot, *Prufrock and Other Observations* (London: Egoist, 1917; rpt London: Faber, 1969) pp. 13–14.

Chapter 4: Emile Zola and the Hyperbole of Consumption

1. Letter on *Germinal* to Henry Céard, 22 March 1885, in Emile Zola, *Oeuvres Complètes*, vol. 14 (containing correspondence), ed. Henri Mitterand (Paris: Cercle du Livre Précieux, 1969) p. 1440.
2. *Le Roman expérimental*, in *Oeuvres Complètes*, vol. 10, ed. Mitterand, p. 1189.
3. Emile Zola, *Germinal*, Pléiade edition of *Les Rougon-Macquart*, vol. 3 (Paris: Gallimard, 1964) p. 1142. All parenthetical page references to Zola's novels are from this edition.
4. See Thomas Hardy, *Jude the Obscure*, Wessex edition (London: Macmillan, 1912) p. 334.
5. Georg Lukács, *Studies in European Realism*, first American edition (New York: Grosset and Dunlap, 1964) p. 45.
6. Ibid., pp. 85–6.
7. See Jean Borie, *Zola et les mythes* (Paris: Editions du Seuil, 1971).

Chapter 5: Thomas Hardy and the Chronic Crisis Syndrome

1. Virginia Woolf, 'The Novels of Thomas Hardy' (1928), in *The Common Reader* (New York: Harcourt Brace, 1948) p. 268.
2. See J. Hillis Miller, *The Disappearance of God* (Cambridge, Mass.: Harvard University Press, 1963).
3. Thomas Hardy, *The Return of the Native*, Wessex edition, vol. 4 (London: Macmillan, 1912) p. 4. All parenthetical page references to Hardy's novels are from this edition.
4. See José Ortega y Gasset, 'The Dehumanization of Art' (Madrid: Revista de Occidente, 1925; trans. Princeton University Press, 1948).
5. In his discussion of the *femme fatale* motif in Romantic literature, Mario Praz quotes Walter Pater's celebrated description of Da Vinci's *Mona Lisa* and comments on the affinity of its profile with *femmes fatales* of Swinburne, Flaubert and Gautier. It is indeed interesting that in the Pater passage, Mona Lisa's 'eyelids are a little weary' and she is depicted as being a virtual culmination of Western culture from Greece, Rome and the Middle Ages to the Renaissance. To some extent, Hardy's heroine also fits into this scheme; the accent in his case, however, would be on her weariness. See Mario Praz, *The Romantic Agony* (1933, rpt London: Fontana Library, 1960) p. 271.
6. As quoted in Florence Emily Hardy, *The Life of Thomas Hardy 1840–1928* (London: Macmillan, 1962) p. 177.
7. In his discussion of the complex irony embodied in the symmetrical patterns of Hardy's prose, J. Hillis Miller makes a pertinent citation of Proust's

commentary on Hardy drawn from Proust, *La Prisonnière*, Pléiade edition, vol. 3 (Paris: Gallimard, 1954) pp. 375–6: he translates it as 'the great writers have never written more than a single work, or rather, they have refracted across diverse milieus that unique beauty which they bring into the world . . . that stone-mason's geometry in [his] novels.' See J. Hillis Miller, *Thomas Hardy: Distance and Desire* (Cambridge, Mass.: Harvard University Press, 1970) pp. 205–7.

8. As quoted in Florence Emily Hardy, *The Life of Thomas Hardy*, pp. 272–3.

Chapter 6: *Joseph Conrad and the Dissolution of an Ethical Code: the Hollow Centre*

1. It is interesting that Ford Madox Ford in his complimentary profile of Conrad should emphasize the writer's cosmopolitan status and associate him thereby with one of the other writers here considered, Henry James. He writes: 'Mr. Conrad, coming from Poland – even as Henry James coming from New England – has once more put Anglo-Saxondom into contact with the main stream of human art [that is, "the European literary tendency"].' See 'Mr. Joseph Conrad and Anglo-Saxondom', in *Thus to Revisit* (New York: Octagon Books, rpt 1966) pp. 101–4. With that 'Western' background, both are indeed qualified to comment on the Western condition. It should be noted that both writers were exposed to continental aesthetics (particularly of France). A study strictly in literary influence could attribute the marked Symbolism of their styles to this fact. Within the context of the present study, the larger socio-aesthetic term of Decadence accounts for such a phenomenon.

2. Letter to George T. Keating, 14 December 1922, in G. Jean-Aubry, *Joseph Conrad: Life and Letters*, vol. 2 (Garden City, NY: Doubleday, 1927) p. 289.

3. Joseph Conrad, Preface to *The Nigger of the 'Narcissus'*, collected edition (London: J. M. Dent, 1950) p. ix. All parenthetical page references to Conrad's novels and tales are from this edition.

4. Hugh Kenner has pointed out in *The Invisible Poet: T. S. Eliot* (New York: McDowell, Obolensky, 1959) p. 147, that originally it was *The Waste Land* that had Conrad's phrase for an epigraph, and that the poem 'The Hollow Men' grew as an appendage (from rejected pieces) of the larger work.

5. In some respects, Conrad seems to be a disciple of the poet who foresook description for atmospheric effect. Mallarmé's notable example was coincidentally 'the horror of the forest', which he substituted for the actual trees which make up the forest – that is, 'the intrinsic and dense wood of the trees'. See 'Variations sur un sujet', in Pléiade edition of Mallarmé's works, *Oeuvres Complètes* (Paris: Gallimard, 1945) pp. 365–6.

6. Vernon Young in his article on *The Nigger of the 'Narcissus'* entitled 'Trial by Water' goes so far as to state that the 'Nigger's' West Indian identity enforces 'the equation of West and Death' – see *Twentieth Century Interpretations of the Nigger*, ed. John A. Palmer (Englewood Cliffs, NJ: Prentice Hall, 1969) p. 27. My own view assumes that the colour of the skin is not racial but symbolic, using a conventional symbolism of darkness for moral transgres-

sion. This becomes transferred to the modern symbolism of whiteness when Conrad paints the livid figure of Kurtz, his ivory face, as a sign of that immorality. It is whiteness which the writer Melville, among others, developed in reference to a metaphysical void – see his *Moby Dick*, *Pierre*, 'Bartleby the Scrivener'. In *The Nigger of the 'Narcissus'*, the darkness demoralizes the Western men and is thereby associated with them. Whereas Conrad demonstrates this as a process, T. S. Eliot takes it as a confirmed state.

7. T. S. Eliot, 'The Hollow Men', *Poems, 1909–1925* (London: Faber & Gwyer, 1925; rpt London: Faber, 1969) p. 83.
8. See my discussion of *The Return of the Native* in Chapter 5, on Thomas Hardy, and the specific reference to the 'modern perceptiveness of the modern type' that Hardy elaborates on.
9. Letter to R. B. Cunninghame Graham, 31 January 1898, in G. Jean-Aubry, *Joseph Conrad: Life and Letters*, vol. 1, p. 226.
10. Letter to William Blackwood, 31 December 1898, in William Blackburn (ed.), *Joseph Conrad: Letters to William Blackwood and David S. Meldrum* (Durham, N. Carolina: Duke University Press, 1958) p. 36.
11. In Spengler's scheme, Kurtz would specifically represent Western culture (which Spengler designated as 'Faustian man') arriving at a stage of 'civilization' which Spengler would class as 'decadent' and Conrad expresses through irony – see Spengler, *The Decline of the West*, vol. 1, pp. 31, 183.
12. Letter to R. B. Cunninghame Graham, 20 December 1897, in G. Jean-Aubry, *Joseph Conrad: Life and Letters*, vol. 1, p. 216.
13. Ibid., p. 216.
14. Using the terms of I. A. Richards – see *The Philosophy of Rhetoric* (New York: Oxford University Press, 1936) and his analysis of metaphor.
15. Psycho-political discussions have been made notably by Eloise Knapp Hay, *The Political Novels of Joseph Conrad* (University of Chicago Press, 1963) and Avrom Fleishman, *Conrad's Politics* (Baltimore: Johns Hopkins University Press, 1967).
16. J. A. Hobson, *Imperialism* (London: Archibald Constable, rev. 1905) p. 10.
17. Jacques Berthoud, *Joseph Conrad: The Major Phase* (Cambridge University Press, 1978) p. 187.

Chapter 7: The Decadent Style

1. William Barrett, 'Existentialism as a Symptom of Man's Contemporary Crisis', in Stanley Romaine Hopper (ed.), *Spiritual Problems in Contemporary Literature* (New York: Harper Torchbooks, 1957) p. 139.
2. György M. Vajda, 'The Structure of the Symbolist Movement', in Anna Balakian (ed.), *A Comparative History of Literature in European Languages*, vol. 2 (Budapest: Akadémiai Kiadó, 1982) p. 29.
3. See David Lodge, *The Language of Fiction* (New York: Columbia University Press, 1966).

4. Zola, *Oeuvres Complètes*, vol. 10, ed. Mitterand, p. 1201.
5. See Gerard Genette, *Narrative Discourse* (Ithaca: Cornell University Press, rpt and trans. (1980).
6. See Tzvetan Todorov, *Poétique de la prose* (Paris: Editions du Seuil, 1971).

Index